FREE TONY HUNTER #333814

Unmasking the Lies That Stole His Freedom

BY:
MRS. EILEEN HUNTER

Publisher Page

Copyright © 2025 by Nuco Enterprise Solutions LLC
All rights reserved.

No portion of this book may be reproduced in any form without written permission from the publisher or author, except as permitted by U.S. copyright law.

This book is **published by Nuco Enterprise Solutions LLC**. First Edition, 2025

Available in **paperback, hardback, audiobook**, and **eBook (Kindle)** editions.

ISBNs:
Paperback: 979-8-218-94242-7
Hardback: 979-8-218-94244-1
Audiobook: 979-8-218-94243-4

For permissions, inquiries, or media requests, please contact: contact@innocentmanconvicted.com

Printed in the United States of America.

Mrs Eileen Hunter is also known as Eileen Durfee and Eileen Durfee Hunter

WHAT EXPERTS ARE SAYING ABOUT FREE TONY HUNTER 333814

"As Tony Hunter's appellate attorney, I reviewed his case in depth and came to believe he is innocent. The book, Free Tony Hunter, is completely accurate and well written. Sadly, too many innocent persons have been sentenced to life in prison based on nothing more than the testimony of clever but soulless jailhouse informants who learn the investigative facts about a crime and then, in exchange for leniency, report to the powers that be having heard—or supposedly overheard—a confession that never occurred. Tony Hunter is the victim of such skullduggery."

— Christopher Aberlee, Attorney, Louisiana Appellate Project.

"Tony Hunter's book isn't just about conviction; it's an urgent look at a human being who must rebuild his life long after the courtroom doors slam shut. As someone who believes in Tony's innocence and in uncovering the truth behind his wrongful conviction, I know how important it is for his story to be told. Tony gives you the unvarnished truth about what the Louisiana criminal justice system doesn't get right, the brutal realities, the search for meaning, and the perseverance required to push back against injustice and hold on to hope. If you want a powerful, honest human story of confronting and unraveling a wrongful conviction, this book is essential reading."

— Kathryn Jakuback Burke, Attorney Longman & Jakuback, APLC

DEDICATION

First and foremost, this book is dedicated to God, my unwavering source of strength. My relationship with Him is deeply rooted, meaningful, and filled with love. Secondly, to my God-sent wife, a warrior strengthener. Life without her would be utterly incomplete. She is an essential part of who I am and everything I do. The happiest moments of my life have been shared with her, filled with spiritual richness and joy.

Tony Hunter

ABOUT THIS BOOK

An innocent man. A triple murder. Three jailhouse informants. One corrupt system.

Louisiana's judicial system wrongfully convicted Tony Hunter #333814 of a triple murder based on the fabricated testimony of three jailhouse informants—no physical evidence, no reliable witnesses, just stories traded for leniency. In a system that values conviction over truth, Tony's life was buried so the state could claim another "win."

This book is Tony's own account of how a corrupt Louisiana criminal justice system twisted lies into a life sentence, and what it feels like to be caged for a crime you did not commit. His story exposes how easily an innocent person can be condemned—and how hard it is to be heard once the gavel falls.

If you believe an innocent man should not die in prison, this book is your invitation to stand with Tony, shine a light on a broken system, and add your voice to the growing demand for justice and reform.

Contents

WHAT EXPERTS ARE SAYING ABOUT FREE TONY HUNTER 333814 iii

DEDICATION iv

ABOUT THIS BOOK v

ACKNOWLEDGMENTS i

LETTER FROM TONY HUNTER.. iii

INTRODUCTION 1

CHAPTER 1: NIGHT OF THE TRIPLE HOMICIDE 10

CHAPTER 2: OTHER WITNESSES 14

CHAPTER 3: THE RED TRUCK 17

CHAPTER 4: CASE GOES COLD – FOCUS SHIFTS TO TONY 19

CHAPTER 5: PROSECUTION OPENING STATEMENT 29

CHAPTER 6: DEFENSE OPENING STATEMENT 36

CHAPTER 7: FRAMING THE INNOCENT: THE COURTROOM DRAMA .. 46

CHAPTER 8: PROSECUTION CLOSING ARGUMENT 53

CHAPTER 9: DEFENSE CLOSING ARGUMENT 58

CHAPTER 10: DECLARATION OF PROFESSOR ROBERT M. BLOOM 86

CHAPTER 11: JERROLD PETERSON'S SUICIDE NOTE 124

ACKNOWLEDGMENTS

This book would not have been possible without the support, guidance, and relentless dedication of many individuals who believed in the importance of Tony Hunter's story.

I would like to express my deepest gratitude to Alex Mahdavian, a remarkable young civil rights activist and aspiring attorney. Alex's involvement in this project began when he first read about Tony's case and was moved by the injustice he faced. Despite the demands of being a college student, Alex devoted countless hours to compiling crucial information, uncovering new insights, and lending his voice to the writing of this book. His passion for justice and his unwavering commitment to exposing the truth have been an inspiration to me and a vital part of this journey.

To all who have supported this endeavor, shared their insights, and encouraged us to press forward—thank you. Your belief in justice and your willingness to stand by Tony's side mean more than words can express. This book is as much a testament to your dedication as it is a record of Tony's resilience.

I also want to extend special thanks to those who contributed to the visual storytelling of this book. Several of the images featured on the front cover help bring Tony's journey to life, and I'm grateful to everyone who helped capture and share those moments.

In particular, I thank *Re-Entry* and *The Angolite* magazine for their powerful photography documenting life inside the Louisiana State Penitentiary at Angola. Your work adds an essential layer of depth and humanity to this story.

LETTER FROM TONY HUNTER

Today is a special day because God has given us the gift of life—a chance to share laughter, love, and gratitude.

I am currently incarcerated for murders I did not commit. Yet even here, I choose to rise above my circumstances. I have completed the Louisiana Department of Corrections' Mentor Certification Training and earned my Criminal Justice Initiative and Moral Compass certifications. As a certified mentor, my goal is simple and deeply personal: to save lives and help others avoid the pain, suffering, and stress I have endured—and continue to face.

Life will always test us through obstacles, circumstances, and challenges. Every day, I face envy, jealousy, and hate. I've poured my loyalty, time, heart, and soul into friendships and relationships, only to be met with betrayal. Those experiences have left me drained mentally and financially. But I've learned—and I want you to learn too—that we don't always have to go through the pain ourselves. We can learn from the testimonies of others.

If I tell you that the bridge is broken, it's because I've fallen off that cliff myself. I'm only alive by God's grace to share the warning. But will you choose to cross that bridge anyway, just to find out for yourself? We can't keep making the same mistakes. We must separate ourselves from people and situations that hold us back and keep us from reaching new levels of growth and purpose.

Yesterday is gone—we can't change it. But right now, at this moment, we are given a choice. A choice to think positively or negatively. No matter what you're going through, you have the power to adjust your mindset so you can overcome life's tests. Always pause and think before you react. Don't let your emotions set you back from building the life you deserve.

Every positive action you take brings you closer to your goals. Be a thinker. Seek wisdom. Speak good things into your life. Surround yourself with people who uplift and motivate you. Invest in your mental growth. Encourage yourself with positive affirmations like: *"I've got this. I can do it."*

Thank you for your time and open mind. Stay strong. Stay focused. And never forget—you are blessed with the gift of life today.

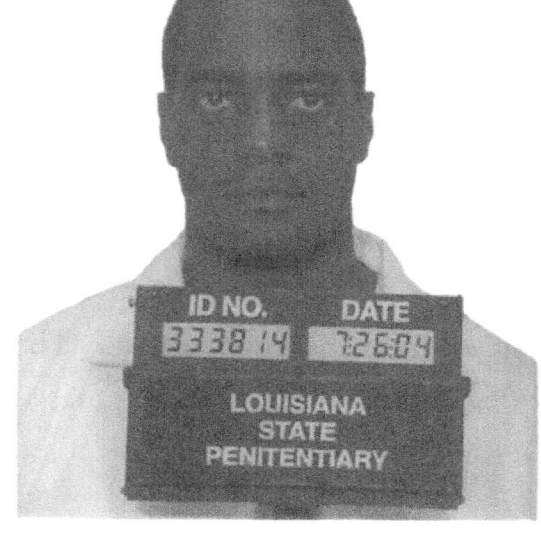

INTRODUCTION

On August 28, 1972, Patricia Hunter gave birth to her son, Tony Hunter, at Conway Hospital in Monroe, Louisiana. Monroe was a city marred by a legacy of racial violence, with the Ku Klux Klan's influence still casting a shadow long after Tony's birth. Although the Civil Rights and Voting Rights Acts had been passed, racial disparities persisted. The War on Drugs had become a weapon to target Black and Brown communities, leading to increased police violence and mass incarceration. Tony and many other young black men became the targets of racist officers who perceived them differently than white individuals, causing a phenomenon of mass incarceration that involved minor crimes and lengthy prison sentences and mostly targeted black and brown Americans.

Until 2019, Tony's home state of Louisiana permitted non-unanimous juries to convict defendants if ten jurors agreed to convict. The rule came into existence in 1898 as Jim Crow legislation thrived throughout the American South, as it was designed to make the conviction of black defendants simpler. Since the Constitution requires a jury of the accused's peers, barring African Americans from jury duty outright was not allowed. Therefore, Louisiana implemented legislation that allowed juries to convict black defendants even if one or two persons of color made it onto the jury. Even though voters abolished the rule, this decision does not apply retroactively, meaning that anyone convicted under this product of Jim Crow remains incarcerated.

Immediately after slavery's abolition, for-profit prisons once again facilitated legal forced servitude. Louisiana State Penitentiary, or Angola, existed originally as a slave plantation during the first half of the nineteenth century. Through the practice of leasing convicts to private companies for cheap labor, Angola and other prisons morphed into substitutes for slavery. As enslavement appeared to fade, this distorted use of the penal system restored much of what slavery entailed. Louisiana has utilized a biased judicial system to provide a steady flow of black prisoners into this system of involuntary servitude. Black Codes and Jim Crow legislation established laws which became the basis on which these men were sentenced to hard labor. Louisiana's legalization of non-unanimous jury convictions is only another in a lengthy list of these racist policies written to harass African Americans. Angola operated as a private prison until the turn of the century, when the state of Louisiana purchased the land, and the facility became Louisiana State Penitentiary. Despite the change in management, the practice of forced labor endured along with reports of various human rights abuses. Today, decades following the Civil Rights Movement, prisoners at Angola continue to provide extraordinarily cheap labor for powerful corporations.

From an early age, Tony had to learn independence and

strength without relying on others. At the age of seven, Tony's mother caught his father unzipping her sister's pants while she slept. She quickly left him and Tony grew up without knowing his father, who never reached out after that. As a single mother, Patricia Hunter did what she could to raise Tony in his father's absence. A hardworking, trustworthy, and faith-driven woman, she instilled her values in Tony from an early age. He adopted her faith and work ethic, using both to propel him forward throughout his troubled youth.

In high school, he found a suitable outlet for his work ethic: sports. Tony excelled as a member of his high school track team, as he imagined a future around his love for athleticism that involved competing professionally. The profound joy of finding something to pour his time and energy into led him to reach new heights, eventually running 200-meters in 21 seconds. The world record, held by Usain Bolt, is 19.19 seconds. Tony saw athletics as his ticket to a more prosperous life; however, this vision was dismantled by a biased criminal justice system.

In 1992, Tony's stepfather, a preacher, allowed him to drive his new Cadillac. Tony and his friends piled into the pristine vehicle and drove around town, during which they picked up a passenger who needed a ride. The nineteen-year-old Tony was overjoyed to be driving the car, a jubilation which quickly turned to fear when a white police officer pulled him over. Without probable cause or any apparent reason, the officer ordered all passengers to exit the car so he could search the vehicle. While an outside perspective can only speculate as to the officer's intentions, it is true that police tend to racially profile minorities because of their skin color. The NYPD's "Stop and Frisk" initiative demonstrated that police often operate based on subconscious prejudices that compel them to view certain individuals as more dangerous. In Tony's case, the appearance of a group of black youths riding in an expensive car explains the officer's haste in ordering them to vacate the car so he could conduct a search. Regardless of his motivation, the officer found that the passenger who had hitched a ride was carrying a rock of cocaine. He confessed that the drugs were his, but the officer arrested Tony.

Tony did not use drugs and had never been in trouble with the law, and he remained confident that everything would be straightened out. He spoke to officers and confirmed that he was only driving the car and knew nothing of the narcotics found on the passenger, who also verified that Tony had nothing to do with it. However, Tony could not afford an attorney. Legal fees are notoriously unaffordable, a reality that left Tony with a public defender. Although laudable profession, being a public defender is an underpaid and overworked position, meaning those who rely on these attorneys as their main line of defense are put at a disadvantage. Tony's public defender urged him to avoid trial and make a confounding decision: plead guilty and face conviction for possession with intent to distribute. This route was enormously unappealing because Tony had not been in possession of the cocaine nor had he any intention of selling it. But there was no other option for Tony, and his only source of legal counseling was telling him that there was nothing else he could do. Staring down the barrel of Louisiana's criminal justice system, Tony reluctantly pleaded guilty and was imprisoned in 1994, leaving his two children.

Now incarcerated, Tony had become the very cautionary tale his mother had warned him about—one he had spent his life trying to avoid. The conviction ignited a surge of rage within him. Despite living a sober, faith-driven life filled with academic and athletic ambitions, he was branded and treated as if he were a depraved criminal. In a single afternoon, his life had been shattered beyond recognition, in ways that were nearly impossible to comprehend.

Trapped in a system designed to incarcerate Black men and prevent them from advancing, Tony faced the harsh reality that freedom would not erase the stigma. Even when he would walk free, the mark of incarceration would continue to deny him access to well-paying jobs and social acceptance.

While serving time, Tony's principles were once again put to the test. He encountered Glen Nelson, a feared inmate known for his violent tendencies, who had cornered another prisoner with the intent to forcibly sodomize him. Tony couldn't stand by. Despite the clear danger, he intervened, stopping Nelson and making it known he would never remain silent in the face of cruelty.

That act of courage came at a high cost. Humiliated and enraged, Glen Nelson set into motion a chain of retaliatory events. What began as a single moment of moral clarity spiraled into a campaign of false accusations and targeted manipulation. That fateful encounter would ultimately contribute to Tony Hunter's eventual life sentence—a cruel twist in a system already rigged against him.

After his release in 1995, Tony set about rebuilding his life, but his criminal record made it hard to find steady work. The situation was made worse when people began confusing him with Frankie Ray Hunter—nicknamed "Trigga"—a man who shared his last name, lived just two blocks away on South Grand Street in Monroe, Louisiana, and had shot and killed his mother's boyfriend. As a result, Tony had to work multiple low-paying jobs to support himself and his family. His time in prison had not offered real benefits like classes or job training, meaning he effectively lost years of progress.

* * * * *

```
State of Louisiana  Vs.  FRANKIE RAY HUNTER JR
Case #:      94-F  -000462        Charge: INF/MANSLAUGHTER
Defendant present, represented by Hon. Michael Courteau, waived formal
arraignment and entered a plea of guilty to Manslaughter. Defendant was sworn
and interrogated by the Court and advised of the agreed to sentence, advised
of the right to plead not guilty or maintain not guilty plea, and have a trial
by judge or jury, advised if trial held of defendant's right against self-
incrimination, advised if defendant did not wish to testify at trial, it would
not be held against him, advised of the right to confrontation, cross-
examination, compulsory process, advised if convicted at trial of defendant's
right to appeal or review by a higher court, advised of the maximum penalty
that could be imposed, and advised of the right to file post conviction relief
within three (3) years and the right to appeal sentence within five (5)days.
Defendant indicated to the Court that he understood said rights and waived
same, also stated that he had conferred with counsel and was satisfied with
representation; realized that he was not obligated to plead guilty and that
defendant's plea was not influenced by any promises, other than what was
stated on the record and no threats were made to defendant for a guilty plea
and realized the Court and no other person would determine defendant's
sentence (see record of interrogation). The Court found the plea to be
knowingly and intelligently entered and accepted said plea. Defendant waived
delays in sentencing and defendant was by the Court sentenced to serve twenty-
one (21) years at hard labor with credit for time served. Defendant
fingerprinted in open court.
```

Tony's experience with incarceration perfectly sums up the systemic forces that perpetuate economic disparities. Black men are both more likely to draw suspicion from police and more likely to be convicted with harsher sentences, meaning they lose out on years of their freedom and exit with less ability to be financially successful. Since crime and drug usage are universally more prevalent in low-income communities, destitute children fall into lifestyles of illegal activity, resulting in their incarceration and subsequent difficulty finding unemployment. This feedback loop explains why recidivism, or the tendency of felons to reoffend after release, is uniquely high in the United States. The reason that "tough on crime" policies fail to achieve their goal is because harsher sentences and more intense policing do not address the root socioeconomic causes of crime. Even those who manage to abstain from negative lifestyles are broadly painted as guilty by association for living in low-class, minority communities, leading to the misguided incarceration of innocent individuals.

On the evening of January 10, 2000, Tony spent the night at a friend's apartment across town. Needing a ride home, he offered $20 to anyone who could take him. Clarence Kennedy stepped up, offering Tony a lift, and Tony, unaware of what was to come, got in the car while at a gas station. Tony handed Clarence the money and waited for his change as they pulled away. It was only two blocks from where they started when Clarence discreetly removed a gun from under his shirt and tucked it beneath the seat.

Moments later, the flashing lights of a police car appeared in the rearview mirror. Clarence, remaining calm, handed Tony a folded stack of bills, which Tony absentmindedly slipped into his pocket. The police pulled them over for expired tags and a broken taillight. Despite these infractions, plus the fact that Clarence didn't have a driver's license, they neither searched the car nor issued Clarence a ticket. Tony, merely a passenger, was asked to step out of the vehicle because he was not wearing a seatbelt. The officers searched him and, to his surprise, arrested him for the seatbelt violation. Clarence, however, was allowed to leave without incident.

At the police station, the true setup revealed itself. When Tony emptied his pockets, officers discovered a rock of cocaine folded inside the money Clarence had given him earlier. Tony, who had never touched drugs and had been simply riding home, found himself caught in a scheme he never saw coming. Despite his innocence, Tony had no choice but to plead guilty. The system had left him without the means to fight back, and Clarence had set him up to take the fall. Once again, Tony was swallowed by the same justice system that had derailed his dreams before. From that first police encounter, his name began circulating in the jailhouse rumor mill—eventually landing in the crosshairs of Glen Nelson and Clarence Kennedy, friends who knew each other well, and who would later retaliate with fabricated stories and false testimony to frame him. After bonding out, Tony ran into Kennedy at the Brown Bag Grocery and confronted him about the setup; from that moment, they were enemies. The animosity that started there grew into the jailhouse lies and courtroom claims that stole Tony's freedom.

To preserve the integrity of future litigation, this book confines itself to the public record and avoids certain details. If you have information—something you saw, heard, or know that could free an innocent man—please come forward and contact Tony's attorneys, Longman & Jakuback, APLC:

Longman & Jakuback, APLC
830 Main Street
Baton Rouge, LA 70802
Office: 2253833644

Your courage matters: it could change a life.

CHAPTER 1

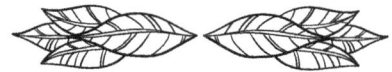

NIGHT OF THE TRIPLE HOMICIDE

The triple homicide at 221 Greenwood Drive ("The Tanglewood Homicides")

On the evening of March 10, 2001, 24-year-old Anthony Rodgers was hosting the opening night for his new nightclub, "Club Daddy's," in Monroe, Louisiana. Earlier that evening, Levi "Chico" Williams, Douglas Simonds, Harold Black and Anthony's 16-year-old godson Henry Staten had left their residence at 221 Greenwood Drive to go to the club to help Anthony with the opening.

Sometime around 11 or 11:30 p.m., the club started to become crowded, and Anthony Rogers sent Douglas Simonds out to get small bills to make change for the cover charge. Simonds left in Rodgers' car and went to two gas stations looking for change but didn't find any. In the meantime, Anthony Rogers sent Levi Williams back to the house at 221 Greenwood Drive, located in the Tanglewood subdivision, to get the small bills out of his safe. The

Tanglewood subdivision was considered a "high crime area" with a lot of break-ins. Henry Staten's 11-year-old brother Chavez Staten and 11-year-old cousin Jeremy Staten were frequent overnight guests at 221 Greenwood Drive and were sleeping over that night. The boys considered Anthony Rodgers to be their "godfather."

Levi Williams left the club driving his white Ford Explorer. After he was unsuccessful in getting change, Douglas Simonds returned to the club. After time had passed and Williams did not return and did not answer his cell phone, Anthony Rogers sent Douglas Simonds and Henry Staten to 221 Greenwood Drive to check on his whereabouts.

When they pulled up to 221 Greenwood, they noticed Chico's white Ford Explorer parked in the yard in front of the door as was his custom. Henry Staten unlocked the front door with his key and immediately saw Chavez and Jeremy lying on the floor, both shot in the head. When Henry Staten saw his brother and cousin, he immediately ran out and called for Douglas Simonds to go inside. Douglas stuck his head inside, immediately saw the boys, and then both he and Henry Staten left to call for help.

Upon hearing of the shootings, Anthony Rogers and about a dozen other people from the club went back to 221 Greenwood Drive. Harold Black armed himself with his .45–caliber pistol, entered the house, and searched for a possible assailant. During their search of the house, the group found Levi Williams lying on the floor of the bedroom, also shot in the head. Chavez Staten, Jeremy Staten and Levi Williams were transported to a nearby hospital. All three victims died from their gunshot wounds.

Ouachita Parish Sheriff's Office ("OPSO") Deputies David Godwin and John Spires were the first officers to respond to the scene. When they pulled up, Harold Black was placing a handgun in the roadway. Deputy Spires secured Harold's pistol and detained him temporarily during the investigation.

The deadbolt on the open front door was in the locked position; however, the door facing was damaged as if it had been forced open. Inside, the investigators identified casings from at least 2 weapons. OPSO investigators recovered live and spent .22 caliber cartridge cases and live and spent .45 caliber cartridge cases on the floor of the house. Deputies also found a box of live .45 caliber cartridges in a desk in Levi Williams' bedroom. The spent .45 caliber shell casings found on the floor were the same brand and caliber as those in the box of live cartridges found in Williams' desk. The deputies observed that the bedroom where Williams' body was located appeared to be ransacked.

During their search of 221 Greenwood Drive, officers located a small safe, three rifles, a set of keys, a set of digital scales and a bag full of what appeared to be marijuana, which were removed from behind a wall in the bathroom.

221 Greenwood was described by Captain Harris as "a major supplier of marijuana in that area." Captain Harris testified that Anthony Rodgers' girlfriend Lashonda Wright informed him that she previously lived at 221 Greenwood Drive and during that time, "she had seen large quantities of money come into the residence being counted. She had observed large quantities of drugs. Quite often if a dealer or a buyer comes into the house while talking to whoever in the house, whether it be Anthony or Chico, ah, they could just sit down and have a bag of marijuana there on the table. They'd roll them a joint and talk about their business."

Lashonda Wright stated that Anthony Rodgers handled the business of money, ordering, purchasing and selling, and Chico handled the business of going to Texas, picking up the drugs, and bringing them back to the Monroe area. Further she said on several occasions she would pool her money in with the other money in order to purchase drugs."

Emma Rogers stated that she had lived at 221 Greenwood up until a few months prior to the homicides. When asked about the drug dealing at the house, Emma Rogers stated that she "didn't know anything about drugs or anything like that." She was adamant that she had no knowledge of the drug distribution going on in the house and had never seen either Chico or Anthony with a handgun.

CHAPTER 2

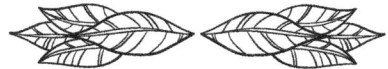

OTHER WITNESSES

On March 11, 2001, Douglas Simonds was interviewed by Sgt. Medaries. Sgt. Medaries asked Douglas Simonds who he thought could have been responsible for what happened. Douglas Simonds responded, "I don't know, we just – people out there saying rumors… supposed to been some dude … it was something like Fat, they call him Fat."

On March 23, 2001, Harold Black was interviewed by Sgt. Medaries. Harold Black told Medaries that he had moved out of 221 Greenwood about two months prior to the homicides "'cause there's nothing, but guys stay there and then because of the drugs, I tell you the truth about that, this situation with drugs, I didn't feel comfortable there, y'know?" Black confirmed that there was a "good amount of drugs in the house."

Medaries asked "do you think that whoever went in there and did that did it to get the drugs or – or money?" and Black responded, "Yes, yes, yes I do - …Yeah, I believe whoever went in that house ... had to be somebody that knew us, knew what was going on, and yes, they did go there for drugs." Black continued: "And I think they killed them two little kids because the kids could identify them. Yes, I do believe that."

The scene at 221 Greenwood was thoroughly processed for potential evidence. Areas around the house where the perpetrator may have been, doorknobs, were dusted for fingerprints, but no usable prints were located. The perimeter of the house was examined for tire tracks or footprints, with no leads. Officers canvassed the neighborhood seeking information, but none of the residents provided any assistance.

On March 17, 2001, a week after the homicides, members of the Monroe Police Department recovered the .22 firearm used to commit the homicides from the median off Hwy 165 near Hadley Street. The serial number was traced to a Randal Smith, who said that he had given the gun to his son, Corey Smith. Corey Smith reported that the gun had been stolen out of his truck in "March or April 2001" while he was parked [at] the Library Lounge. Smith testified that he did not file a police report because he didn't have the serial number. The handgun was tested for fingerprints, and "there were no latent [fingerprints] on the weapon that would connect it to Tony Hunter...".

On March 26, 2001, Anthony Rodgers was interviewed again. Investigators informed him that they had received an anonymous tip that advised that drugs were being sold out of his residence at 221 Greenwood Drive. Anthony Rodgers, told Captain Harris that Williams was "very secretive with his business and did not discuss it." Rodgers was unable to identify anyone – buyers or sellers – who were involved with Williams but said that Williams had received a shipment of 20 to 25 lbs. of marijuana approximately one week prior to the homicides.

At Tony Hunter's bond reduction hearing, Detective Harris testified that "[Anthony Rodgers] never had any links to Tony Hunter. Never said he knew him, you know, as far as knowing him, business with him in there, did not."

Anthony Rodgers later refused to testify at the trial for his godsons' murders, informing the court that if he was called, he would assert his Fifth Amendment privilege.

CHAPTER 3

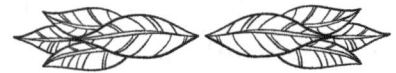

THE RED TRUCK

Two days after the homicides, Anthony Rogers' sister, Emma Rodgers told the police that on the night of the homicides, she left her job as a cashier at the Shell Station on DeSiard Street at 10 p.m. She briefly stopped by her house on Parkview Drive and then proceeded to her mother's house at 409 Greenwood Drive to pick her children up. Her mother's house is four or five houses from 221 Greenwood Drive. When she passed 221 Greenwood, she did not see any vehicles, so she decided not to stop.

She picked up her kids, who were asleep, from her mother's house and loaded them into her car. She testified she only stayed for five minutes because she was "ready to go." When she drove back by 221 Greenwood, she noticed Chico's off-white Ford Explorer truck parked in front of the door. She didn't notice any lights on, so she didn't stop and kept driving.

Emma Rodgers told the police that when she was driving on Greenwood, she observed a truck driving real slow past her headed in the opposite direction. She noticed the truck because it was driving slow and the bottom left headlight was out. She described the truck as a red extended cab with dark tinted windows and that the truck had a double-lamp setup at the bottom, and one of those lamps was not working. She did not notice any of the occupants. She thought to herself that if she had been driving without a working headlight, she would have gotten a ticket, but this guy is getting away with it. She said she had never seen the truck in the area before.

On March 26, 2001, Rodgers told police that about a week after the homicides she was sitting at the Shell Station by the register, right by the window, and looked up and saw "Trigger" in a red truck looking at her. She stated that he was driving a new red truck and that it was the same one she saw on Greenwood Drive the night of the homicides, a shiny red extended cab pick-up truck with tinted windows. She had seen "Trigger" before on several occasions but had never seen him driving a red truck.

CHAPTER 4

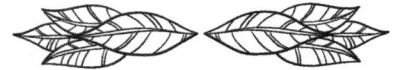

CASE GOES COLD – FOCUS SHIFTS TO TONY

No physical evidence or witnesses; the case goes cold.

Captain Harris personally canvassed Tanglewood Subdivision and not a single person reported hearing or seeing anything related to the homicides on March 10, 2001. He specifically asked neighbors if they heard gunshots, and no one reported hearing anything. Harris testified: "when I hit the streets, I did a canvas of the entire neighborhood down at Tanglewood. I tell the people there was a lot of money out on the board for information. You tell me who did it, you know same as crime stoppers. Said, plus Crime Stoppers is offering a reward. And if I'm not mistaken, ah, I don't recall if it ever was aired on Crime Stoppers, but that was the way that information was put out, that needed witnesses. I needed anybody that would talk to me, and I was running into a brick wall because nobody would talk." At the bond hearing, Captain Harris was asked: "So you offered some financial incentive in exchange for information to help you resolve the case?" He responded, "Yes sir. Cash money." The OPSO offered reward money in addition to the $2000 crime stoppers was offering for information about the homicides.

On March 11, 2002, the local newspaper printed an article titled: "Triple homicide unsolved a year later." Maj. Pat Willis told the paper that "the Sheriff's Office feels confident about who they believe was responsible for the shooting." The paper reported that investigators had previously stated that an arrest would be made by the end of 2001. Willis said he wouldn't "be satisfied with 2001 until the triple homicide is solved, " but that "leads in the case have totally dropped off. For some reason, no one is wanting to come forward. This is a difficult case to get anyone to talk to us about."

OUACHITA PARISH SHERIFF OFFICE

In March 2001, when the homicides occurred, Tony Hunter was living with his girlfriend Stephanie Stokes and their four children in an apartment at 55 Colonial Manner.

He was employed as a welder's helper at James Machine Works. His supervisor at James Machine Works, Ronald Davidson, testified that Tony Hunter worked a full week during the week of March 5-10, 2001, except for Thursday the 8th which was a day off, and a full 39-hour week the following week, March 12-16, 2001.

On March 7, 2001, Tony Hunter had leased a red 2000 Ford F-150 pick-up truck with an extended cab from Enterprise to get back and forth from work. That night, Sgt. Hawkins of the OPSO conducted a traffic stop of Tony Hunter in the red Ford F-150 and issued him citations for driving 34 mph in a 15-mph zone and for having open container. Notably, the traffic stop occurred at 10:47 p.m., the day he leased a new truck and three days before the homicides, and Hunter was not cited for having a malfunctioning headlight.

Three days later, on March 10, 2001, Tony Hunter brought his 11-year-old daughter, Porcia to a party for all of the March birthdays on South 1st Street hosted by Brenda Graves, until about 7:30 p.m. He returned with Porcia to the apartment he shared with Stephanie Stokes, the mother of his four younger children, in Monroe. Stephanie Stokes remembered it was still light out when Tony and Porcia returned because her younger children wanted to play outside with their father and big sister, and they did. Stephanie Stokes specifically remembered this night because the following day was their son Tony Jr.'s birthday and Porcia spent the night to help get ready for Tony Jr.'s party. Stephanie remembered the tv being on because Tony always liked to watch the 10 o'clock news.

Almost two months later, on May 4, 2001, Tony Hunter was arrested for unauthorized use of a moveable in connection with failing to return the red Ford F-150 pick-up truck he had rented from Enterprise on his credit card. When he was arrested, Lamont Smiley was driving the F-150 and Tony Hunter was riding in the passenger seat.

On May 10, 2001, investigators processed the red F-150. The front seats and carpet were processed with Luminal. The upholstery and carpet were vacuumed for hairs, fibers, and blood. The results all came back negative. Detective Harris testified that when he examined the red truck a few days after it was seized it had two functioning headlights (see footnote on page 74) with only a factory tint. The F-150 was thoroughly processed for possible evidence.

Various items of Tony Hunter's clothing were collected from his Colonial Manner apartment including a sweater and a shirt that "appeared to have blood stains on them." They were sent out for processing at Gene Screen and came up with negative results.

On May 6, 2001, Tony Hunter was interviewed by Detective Harris at the Ouachita Correctional Center. Tony Hunter was read and waived his *Miranda* rights. He told the Detective that he did not know Levi Williams or the two children and that he had never been to 221 Greenwood Drive. He adamantly denied being involved in the murders, stating that he had five of his own children and would never hurt a child. He offered to take a lie detector test to prove his innocence.

Brenda Graves was interviewed on May 8, 2001. She stated that Tony Hunter attended a neighborhood birthday party on March 10, 2001, with his daughter Porcia (then 11–12 years old) and remained there until at least 7:30 p.m. She told investigators she did not see him after 7:30 p.m.

On June 12, 2001, KTVE aired multiple stories announcing that Tony Hunter had been arrested for the murder of Roderick Hall and that investigators believed Tony Hunter also had involvement in the Tanglewood homicides.

> **Suspect**
> ■ Willis says he believes they have the right suspect.
>
> From page 3A
>
> Tony L. Hunter, 28, of Monroe, was charged June 12 in connection with Hall's murder. Police did not have to pick Hunter up because he was already being held at the Ouachita Parish Jail on unrelated charges.
>
> "We now believe we have the right suspects," Willis said.
>
> He said Nelson should be considered armed and dangerous.
>
> Nelson is described as approximately 5-foot-9-inches tall and 160 pounds. Willis said the suspect is believed to be driving a brown 1985 Oldsmobile, with low profile tires and chrome rims.
>
> Anyone with information leading to the Nelson's arrest should call their local authorities or the Ouachita Parish Sheriff's Office at 329-1200.

In the weeks after KTVE aired stories linking Tony Hunter to the Tanglewood triple homicide, jailhouse informants at the Ouachita Parish Correctional Center—housed alongside Tony—began seeking out investigators and offering statements against him. Those snitch informants included: Vaccara Comanche (July 20, 2001), Christopher Wiggins (August 2, 2001), and Clarence Kennedy (August 20, 2001).

Months after Comanche, Kennedy, and Wiggins provided their recorded statements to investigators, Tony Hunter had still not been arrested for the triple homicides in Tanglewood.

On February 2, 2002, the State received the January 30, 2002, Gene Screen report that excluded Hunter from being tied to the murder scene, the victims, and the murder weapon.

On February 13, 2002 the State filed a Motion to Dismiss Kennedy's *Simple Burglary* charge, due to a "Plea Deal", yet during trial (page 592 of the Trial Transcript) Kennedy confirms that "Simple Burglary" was one of his convictions, instead of telling the truth and revealing it was dismissed; otherwise, Kennedy had no Simple Burglary charge on record.

```
STATE OF LOUISIANA    *   PARISH OF OUACHITA   *   FOURTH JUDICIAL DISTRICT COURT
STATE OF LOUISIANA                                 FILED:    FEB 13 2002
VS 01-F0948B
KENNEDY, CLARENCE                                  BY:  _____
 (0001902F)                                             DEPUTY CLERK OF COURT
    ARRESTING AGENCY NO. 00-13508

CT. 1     SIMPLE BURGLARY

                       MOTION TO DISMISS

        THIS PROSECUTION HAVING BEEN INSTITUTED BY BILL OF INFORMATION,
FILED JUNE 8, 2001 AGAINST DEFENDANT, KENNEDY, CLARENCE, IS HEREBY
DISMISSED IN ACCORDANCE WITH ARTICLE 691 OF THE LOUISIANA CODE OF
CRIMINAL PROCEDURE.

        MONROE, OUACHITA PARISH, LOUISIANA, THIS  12TH  DAY OF
  February        , 20 02 .


                                            _____
                                            ASSISTANT DISTRICT ATTORNEY

    DISMISSED CASE PER PLEA TO 01-F0649B.  PER GSA
```

On March 5, 2002, the State filed a Motion to Dismiss Comanche's Possession of Cocaine (Schedule II) charge, which was not disclosed at trial and the Prosecution withheld the information from the Defense.

```
STATE OF LOUISIANA  *  PARISH OF OUACHITA  *  FOURTH JUDICIAL DISTRICT COURT
STATE OF LOUISIANA                                FILED:      MAR 0 5 2002
VS  00-F0303B
COMANCHE, VACCARA AKA VACARA BROWN                BY: _____
(0000349F)                                             DEPUTY CLERK OF COURT
ARRESTING AGENCY NO. 00-2739

CT. 1    POSSESSION OF COCAINE (SCHEDULE II)

                        MOTION TO DISMISS

        THIS PROSECUTION HAVING BEEN INSTITUTED BY BILL OF INFORMATION,
FILED MARCH 1, 2000 AGAINST DEFENDANT, COMANCHE, VACCARA AKA VACARA
BROWN, IS HEREBY DISMISSED IN ACCORDANCE WITH ARTICLE 691 OF THE
LOUISIANA CODE OF CRIMINAL PROCEDURE.

        MONROE, OUACHITA PARISH, LOUISIANA, THIS    5    DAY OF
  March   , 20 02 .

                                       _____
                                       ASSISTANT DISTRICT ATTORNEY

DISMISSED CASE PER CONVICTION AND SENTENCED IN 00-F1473
AND 00-F1474. PER GSA
```

On March 11, 2002, the local newspaper printed an article titled "Triple homicide unsolved a year later." The article revealed pertinent details about the homicides, including the names of the victims, where they were found, that a .22 caliber handgun was the murder weapon, and that OPSO was desperate for information on the case. Without any forensic or physical evidence to suggest the perpetrator of the murders, pressure mounting to solve the case, and time passing without any developing leads, investigators doubled back to Tony Hunter.

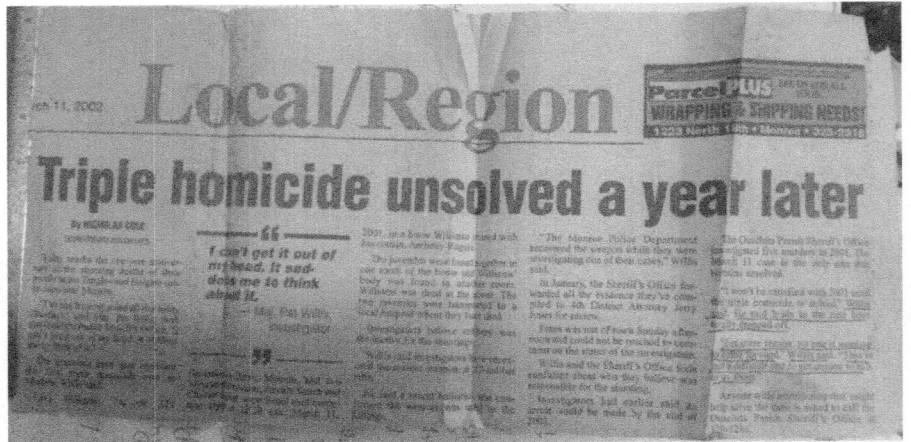

On October 17, 2002, nineteen months after the homicides and over 12 months after three jailhouse informants gave recorded statements implicating him, Tony Hunter was indicted for the Second-Degree Murders of Chavez Staten, Jeremy Staten, and Levi Williams and a single count of Armed Robbery.

FREE TONY HUNTER #333814

Nelson's statements to police will be allowed, judge rules

By CHRISTY FUTCH
cfutch@thenewsstar.com

Fourth District Judge Benjamin Jones denied a defense motion to suppress a second-degree murder defendant's statements to police.

Glen Dale Nelson testified on the stand that he made statements to police — one of them allegedly self-incriminating — because police officers promised he would "walk" on the charges if he helped build a case against Tony Hunter, Nelson's co-defendant in the shooting.

Both Nelson and Hunter are charged with the 2000 shooting death of Roderick Hall of Monroe.

Hunter, 31, Monroe, is charged with three counts of second-degree murder and armed robbery in connection with an unrelated shooting in Tanglewood subdivision in March of 2001. In that incident, two 11-year-old cousins, Jeremy and Chavez Sturns and 24-year-old Levi Williams were all found shot to death.

Nelson, who is also charged with accessory after the fact in connection with a triple homicide, testified that police were looking for evidence against Hunter, and threatened to put the two together in a cell.

Nelson's defense attorney, Louis G. Scott, argued that the statement was not given voluntarily because Nelson was being pressured by authorities, was made promises to be released in exchange for the information, and his attorney was not present when the statements were taken.

First Assistant District Attorney Stephen Sylvester argued that both representatives from his office and the Ouachita Parish Sheriff's Office met with Nelson at Nelson's request.

Nelson will appear in court March 8 for hearings.

Tony Hunter is scheduled to appear today in 4th District Court.

CHAPTER 5

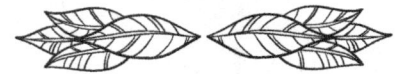

PROSECUTION OPENING STATEMENT

This chapter reprints the official trial transcript. Wording and grammar errors have been intentionally preserved to reflect what occurred in court.

Thank you, Your Honor. May it please the Court, ladies and gentlemen of the jury, the evidence in this case is going to show you that Tony Hunter, also known as "Trigger," is a cold, calculating, and to some extent a very smart murderer. Levi Williams, also known as "Chico," died because "Trigger" wanted something. Chavez and Jeremy Staten died because they were there and they would be able to identify Tony Hunter.

On March the 11th, 2001, about 12:30 in the morning Deputy John Spires, with the Ouachita Parish Sheriff's Office, was dispatched and arrived at 221 Greenwood, located in the Tanglewood Heights subdivision of Ouachita Parish. The first thing he noticed when he pulled up, there was a gentleman standing at the end of the driveway at 221 Greenwood with a pistol in his hand. Obviously, the deputy was concerned. He went and talked to this individual who turned out to be Harold Black. The deputy found a .45 automatic that was lying on the street. The action of the gun was open; the magazine was out and there was a live Federal .45 caliber bullet on the ground. This was Harold Black's gun. Harold had heard about the shootings. He went to 221 Greenwood, and he brought the gun for protection. As it's going to turn out, and the evidence will show, this gun had nothing to do with anything that occurred at 221 Greenwood.

Right behind Deputy Spires was Deputy David Godwin. When he saw Deputy Spires talking to Mr. Black, he was notified that he needed to go inside and check that there were people injured. He entered the residence at 221 Greenwood, and when he did, to his right was a child lying on the floor with blood all around him. To his left at the beginning of a hallway he saw the legs of another child. Sitting next to that child was Pam Staten, the mother of Jeremy Staten. At this time Deputy Johns attempted to get the EMS people in and the paramedics in and he made a protective sweep of the residence. When he made the sweep of the residence he located another victim, Levi Williams, "Chico," in the back bedroom. "Chico" was dead. He also noticed at that time that the bedroom that "Chico" was in looked like it had been ransacked. OPSO supervisors were notified, and they arrived at the crime scene along with the crime scene unit. Levi Williams, Jr., was pronounced dead at the scene. Chavez and Jeremy Staten were not dead. They were taken to the hospital, and they were later pronounced dead at the hospital. Among the other wounds that they had, all three were shot in the head. As it turns out, the primary residents of 221 Greenwood were Anthony Rodgers, Henry Staten and Levi "Chico" Williams. Other people stayed there from time to time including Doug Simons and Harold Black.

Now, all this started on Saturday night of March the 10th. Anthony Rodgers was opening a new club located at 165 and Ticheli. "Big Daddy's," I think, is what it was called. Harold Black was helping him get the club open, so was Doug Simons. Even Henry Staten, who at that time was sixteen years old, was assisting by bringing lights and stuff to the club. Sometime that night, Anthony, also known as "Ant," realized that he needed some type of change to make change for the people that were coming in the residence. First Doug Simons went to try to get some change, but because it was getting kind of late, he was unable to. So, then "Chico" was sent back to 221 Greenwood to get some change.

Well, "Chico" didn't come back for a little while, so Anthony became concerned and he sent Henry and Doug Simons to this residence to try to locate him. When they got there, Henry Staten opened the door with his key, and when he opened the door, he saw his brother and his cousin lying on the floor. He went to check on them, he saw blood around the bodies, so he ran outside and told Mr. Simons. Doug Simons likewise came into the residence, saw these two individuals on the floor and they immediately left. There was no phone there. They immediately left to try to find help. They were trying to get somebody on the cell phone and ultimately, they flagged down, I believe, a Richwood police officer and told them they needed help at this address. They went back to the club, and they told Anthony and Pam Staten what had happened. Several members of the club went back to the residence and went in the residence.

It turns out that there was a little safe and some money that was in the safe that was gone from the house. Once the crime scene unit arrived and began processing the scene they found signs of forced entry at the front door. It appeared that the door had been forcibly opened, the dead bolt was still all the way to the right as in a locked position. But where the door facing was with the dead bolt was broke open.

Inside the residence the investigators found live .22 shell bullets on the floor. They found spent .22 shell bullets on the floor. They found live .45 Spere Brand bullets on the floor and empty Spere Brand .45 bullets on the floor. There was also what appeared to be bullet holes in the wall. And they'll describe to you what they saw inside the house and what they didn't see inside the house.

Now, Emma Rodgers, she's the sister of Anthony Rodgers, she worked at that time at a Shell Stop and Save on DeSiard. When she got off work that night, sometime after 10:30, she proceeded to Greenwood to pick up her children that were staying actually, I believe, two doors down from 221. As she was leaving Greenwood, she observed a truck that was driving real slow. It caught her attention. The truck she described as seeing was a red extended cab pickup truck. Really didn't think a whole bunch about it till about a week later while she was working an individual pulled up at the store on DeSiard and sat in the truck. The truck was a red extended cab pickup truck, and the person that was driving this truck was Tony Hunter.

Now after this happened, members of OPSO...put out a statewide teletype if any agencies came up with a .22 caliber pistol, they wanted to be notified. About a week after March the 10th, 2001 they were notified that Monroe P.D. had found an automatic .22 pistol in the median of 165. This gun was turned over [to] the members of the Ouachita Parish Sheriff's Office. It was sent for analysis and compared to the bullets that were found at 221 Greenwood, and that were found in the heads of these victims. This was the gun that killed them. Now, further in their investigation they did a trace of this .22 caliber pistol [and] found out that it was sold sometime in 1992 by Outfitters to a man named Randall Smith that lives in Sterlington. It turns out that Randall Smith had loaned the gun or given the gun to his son, Corey Smith, and that the gun had been stolen from his pickup truck, or he found it missing from his pickup truck on January the 11th, 2001.

On May the 4th, 2001 Tony Hunter was contacted while he was an occupant of a 2002 Ford F150 extended cab red pickup truck that he had leased from Enterprise Leasing. The truck was processed but there was nothing that was found in the truck that linked Tony Hunter to the crime scene itself. You'll hear that the crime scene unit did not recover any usable prints from inside 221 Greenwood, and also that that's not unusual. And that they also did not come up with any type of other physical evidence that would link the inside of 221 Greenwood to Tony Hunter.

So, basically at this time the sheriff's office had run up into a brick wall. They had no physical evidence from the inside of the residence to link them to Tony Hunter and, although they had the gun that was used, they had no evidence that linked it to Tony Hunter as well. But then again, Tony Hunter showed how cold, calculating, and to some extent how smart he was, or how smart he thought he was. The evidence that you'll hear in this courtroom will not only place Tony Hunter at 221 Greenwood on the night of March the 10th, 2001, it will place him inside 221 Greenwood on the night of March the 10th, 2001.

And not only will you hear why Levi Williams, Jr. was killed, but you'll also hear why these two kids were killed. Because they were the only witnesses, he thought, to Tony Hunter. During the course of these proceedings, you will probably hear evidence and reach a conclusion that Tony Hunter did not act alone. That's fine. The State's not contending otherwise. But we're only here today and you're only here this week to concern yourself about Tony Hunter and not with anybody else.

I'm convinced after you hear - heard all the evidence in this case and evaluate the same that you will be convinced beyond a reasonable doubt that Tony Hunter is guilty of three counts of second-degree murder and one count of armed robbery. Thank you.

* * *

Tony internally recoiled at every word. Cold. Calculating. He was immediately shocked by the artistic liberties taken to construct the narrative. He looked over at his public defender, who gathered a few papers and stood up to the podium.

CHAPTER 6

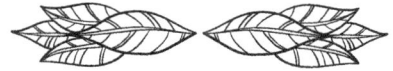

DEFENSE OPENING STATEMENT

This chapter reprints the official trial transcript. Wording and grammar errors have been intentionally preserved to reflect what occurred in court.

May it please the Court, Judge Manning, the Court's personnel, Counsel for the State, co-counsel for the accused Mr. Hunter, ladies and gentlemen of the jury, good morning. As you know my name is Robert Johnson and I, along with my co-counsel in this case, Mr. Bobby Manning, have the privilege of representing the accused in this case, Tony Hunter.

Mr. Hunter is the individual, as you know, who is seated with us at counsel table. As Mr. Ruddick has indicated, he is charged in this prosecution with three counts of second degree murder and one count of armed robbery. A short while ago the Deputy Clerk of Court in this case read to you the Bill of Indictment charging those crimes. Immediately thereafter the State's attorney, Mr. Ruddick, got up and he made to you his opening statements. In it, he outlined to you the nature of the government's case and the nature of the evidence by which they expect to prove that case.

I would caution you here, ladies and gentlemen, on two points. First, the Bill of Indictment that was read to you by the Deputy Clerk of Court is not and should not be considered by you as evidence. In Louisiana there are three methods by which a criminal prosecution may be instituted or started. One of which is a Bill of Indictment, which is nothing more or less than a written accusation of guilt signed by the Grand Jury foreperson and filed into court. It is not and should not be considered by you as evidence. The second and final point I want to make to you here is that the opening statements of the attorneys in this case is not and should not be considered by you as evidence. You notice when I came before you, and when Mr. Ruddick came before me, that he was not sworn as a witness and neither was I. That's for a very simple reason, ladies and gentlemen. We are not witnesses in this case but merely advocates for our respective clients. In this case Mr. Ruddick and the rest of the prosecution team on behalf of the State, and myself and the rest of the defense team on behalf of the accused Tony Hunter.

Therefore, nothing that we say here in our opening comments or remarks is or should be considered by you as evidence. The only evidence that you can lawfully and rightfully consider during the course of this prosecution is the live testimonial evidence that comes to you under oath from that witness stand, any items of physical evidence that are offered and introduced during the course of the trial, and any lack of evidence that you may find after you have considered, analyzed and thought about this case and discussed it with your fellow jurors during your deliberation process. That is the only evidence, ladies and gentlemen, that you can consider in arriving at whatever verdict that you arrive at in this case.

Now, since this is a criminal prosecution, as you know, the burden rests entirely and squarely on the shoulders of the State to prove the guilt of the accused beyond a reasonable doubt. That is to say they must prove each and every element of each and every crime that is listed in the Bill of Indictment before you can return a verdict in this case. And, of course, if they fail to prove each and every element of each and every crime that is listed in the Bill of Indictment you have a sworn duty under oath and the law to find the accused not guilty.

Now, the accused in this case is presumed innocent, and he also carries a Fifth Amendment Privilege not to take the witness stand and testify. The same right or privilege that you or a member of your family would have if you all were on trial here today and charged with the very same crimes that Mr. Hunter is charged with. Furthermore, the defendant is not required to present any evidence. And the law states that since the defendant is not required to make a—is not required to take the witness stand and that he is presumed innocent it follows a logical sequence, ladies and gentlemen, that the defendant likewise does not have to make an opening statement. But, the law states that if we elect to make an opening statement, as we have in this case, then we're restricted by law to explaining to you the nature of our defense and the nature of the evidence by which we expect to prove that defense so that you the members of the jury can more easily follow that evidence as it unfolds during the course of this trial. Now, at the outset of these proceedings Mr. Hunter appeared in court for what is known as his arraignment session of court where he was called upon to enter one of several pleas that may be entered in connection with criminal prosecution in Louisiana. When his name was read on the docket he stood and through counsel entered a plea of not guilty. In entering that plea, ladies and gentlemen, Tony Hunter was saying to the Court, to the State of Louisiana, to the world that he is not guilty of these charges or any of the lesser and included offenses that make up this charge, or these charges rather. Having entered that plea, his case was trial bound and that's why we're here for that trial.

Why did Tony Hunter enter those pleas? He entered those pleas because he is not guilty of these offenses. What is his defense in this particular case? The oldest defense known in the law, someone other than Mr. Hunter committed these crimes. How will we establish this defense? Well, contrary to what the government has said to you in its opening remarks, ladies and gentlemen, we expect the evidence to show that the accused, Tony Hunter, is thirty-one years of age. That he is single. He is the father of five children, and at the time that these crimes occurred that he was gainfully employed by James Machine Works, a local business establishment located on DeSiard as a welder's helper.

We expect the evidence to further show that the week of these homicides that Mr. Hunter worked a full forty hour work week. We expect the evidence to show that the week following these homicides that Mr. Hunter went back to work and again worked a full forty hour work week with his employer. We expect the evidence to show that on the night—ah, on Friday night and early Saturday morning and into the evening that Tony Hunter attended a party. That he was seen at this party. The party was given by friends of his, Brenda and John Graves, and Florica Greene. We expect the evidence to show that Tony Hunter was at that party. We'll have witnesses who will come in and say that. That he was seen at the party throughout the night. We expect the evidence to show, ladies and gentlemen, that Mr. Hunter learned about these crimes the same time the general public learned about it through news accounts that were published of this - about these crimes in the News Star World, KNOE-TV, and TV-10.

We expect the evidence to show that shortly after these homicides were committed that there was word or rumor in the gossip columns and the rumor mills that Mr. Hunter may have been connected with them. At that time Mr. Hunter did the responsible and the civic thing that any of us would have done, he contacted David Harris, Captain David Harris who has been listed both as a State's witness as well as a defense witness. He contacted Detective

Harris. He said, "I understand that you have rumors or people are telling you that I'm involved with these crimes." He says, "in order to set the record straight and to clear my name I want to come in. I'll do anything to help you solve these cases. I want to come in. I'll take a lie detector test, and of course anything meaning give you a DNA sample, whatever it takes in order to clear my name so that you won't waste any time focusing on me and you can get back to the business at hand, and that is of trying to find the people who actually committed these crimes." He made that offer to Detective Harris. Detective Harris' response, "well, I'm not prepared for you to come in at this time. Don't come in." That's what happened, and that's what the evidence will show, and Detective Harris will tell you that.

But, the offer was laid on the table and it was placed there by Mr. Hunter. Detective Harris did not contact Mr. Hunter. Mr. Hunter contacted Detective Harris. The evidence will further show that even after his incarceration in connection with this case that Mr. Hunter continued to be cooperative with law enforcement. The evidence will show that he made certain statements and at the end of those statements he indicated, "listen, why you all focusing on me? You ought to be trying to find out or deal with the drug dealers in the area. The people who are really responsible for these crimes." The evidence—why did Mr. Hunter make that statement? The evidence will show, as Mr. Ruddick indicated, that the residence where these crimes were committed was occupied by one Anthony

Rodgers, Levi "Chico" Williams as well as Henry Staten. The evidence will show that both Mr. Rodgers as well as Mr. Williams dealt large quantities of drugs out of 221 Greenwood Drive. As a matter of fact, a shipment of marijuana in the amount of twenty to twenty-five pounds had come into the residence a week or so before this incident occurred, and that there was evidence that they thought that that shipment had been distributed either by Mr. Rodgers or Mr. Williams prior to the time that these homicides were committed. The evidence will show that in the eyes of the law enforcement community here in Ouachita Parish that 221 Greenwood Drive was a major distribution center for marijuana and possibly cocaine. The evidence will show further that after these crimes were committed that there was in fact an investigation that was conducted by the crime scene unit of Ouachita Parish Sheriff's Office. The evidence will further show that during their very detailed and their very comprehensive and their very exhausted search of that residence that no fingerprints of the accused were found in that residence. They will—the evidence will show that no hairs, no fibers were found in that residence that link Tony Hunter to that residence.

The evidence will show that no DNA of Tony Hunter's was left in that residence. The evidence will show that the alleged murder weapon that was subsequently found on 165 was not connected to Tony Hunter. The evidence will show with regard to the truck that was seized and allegedly—and driven by Mr. Hunter, that that particular truck was processed very thoroughly by all of the law enforcement officers that were involved in that process. They took from the truck upholstery samples. They took carpet samples and every other sample imaginative from that truck in an effort to try to find some trace evidence. Some type of blood, some type of hair, some type of fibers from the truck that would match to the crime scene or match Tony Hunter to the crime scene or any of these victims in this case, and they found nothing. Nothing, ladies and gentlemen. And that's what the evidence will show.

Now, you may hear other evidence in the course of this trial, but we submit to you, ladies and gentlemen, that after you have heard all of the evidence in this case, and I ask that you keep an open mind and listen to all of the evidence. But, after you have heard all of the evidence during the course of this trial, ladies and gentlemen, we submit to you that you find that the case—that the State's case is wanting in quantity and wanting in quality, and wanting in sufficient evidence to find the accused not guilty—guilty of any of these crimes.

And therefore, we will come to you, ladies and gentlemen, at the close of this trial. We will remind you of the oath that you took at the beginning of this trial. That oath being that you would try this case in a just and impartial manner and render a verdict in accordance with the law and the evidence that the judge will give to you, which we submit, ladies and gentlemen, can only be a verdict of finding the accused, Tony Hunter, not guilty. I thank you for your time and your attention.

* * *

Tony's eyes met Johnson's briefly before Judge Manning interrupted: "Counsel approach." Johnson quickly threw his papers back onto the defense table and approached the Judge's bench along with Ruddick. They whispered to each other momentarily before Manning shooed them away with his hand.

"Ladies and gentlemen," Judge Manning declared, "having completed the opening statements, we're going to recess for lunch. When we return from lunch, the State will begin its case in chief with testimony. I'm going to remind you that while you're gone from the courtroom you are not to discuss the case nor permit it to be discussed in your presence. We will resume with testimony at 1:00 o'clock. Also during this time avoid any news media accounts relative to the case. Includes TV., radio or newspaper, any other source of information behind what is said in this courtroom to you in the way of testimony. Do you understand my instructions?"

The jury nodded and mumbled accordingly before being herded back into the deliberation room. Judge Manning looked at his watch, "All right. We'll see you back here—"

"I have one matter, Your Honor." Ruddick stood abruptly. "Once we were coming back from the bench conference, there was a lady that came in with three children, and they began waving at Mr. Hunter, and he began waving at them." Tony sat up and stiffened his back.

Judge Manning responded, "please, ladies and gentlemen, those who are here as spectators, there should be no outward expression of any emotion, no talking to the defendant or any of the witnesses. No hand gestures of any kind. Can I have the assurance from ladies and gentlemen in the courtroom?"

Spectators around the courtroom started speaking to each other, the orderly nature of the room falling apart. Johnson began, "you have our assurance from my client—"

Ruddick turned to Tony and interjected, "Mr. Johnson is not being instructed, Mr. Manning is not being instructed, but rather Tony Hunter is being instructed not to turn around and start waving at these people."

A surge of murmurs erupted from behind Tony. Judge Manning adjourned the Court.

CHAPTER 7

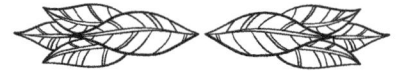

FRAMING THE INNOCENT: THE COURTROOM DRAMA

Tony's trial juror members consisted of seven white women, three white men, one black woman, and one black man. Alternate jury members consisted of one white man and one white woman. The prosecutions strategy was to appeal to the women on the jury, as studies suggest have a heightened emotional response to cases involving children. By leveraging this emotional connection, the prosecution aimed to foster a sense of moral outrage and urgency, making it more challenging for jurors to separate their feelings from the factual evidence presented in the trial.

In Tony's murder trial the prosecution employed a strategy that played on the emotional response of the jury, particularly by displaying photos of the two children who were tragically murdered. This tactic aimed to evoke deep feelings of sympathy and outrage which could sway the jury's perception of the case. The emotional appeal was designed to elicit a visceral reaction, potentially overshadowing the evidentiary weakness in the prosecution's case.

The prosecution built its case primarily on the testimonies of three jailhouse informants, individuals who claimed to have overheard Tony talking to Glen Nelson through a protective, double-thick, shatter proof, glass window. A testing of the window will prove that it is scientifically impossible to hear a conversation through that double-thick, shatter proof glass window as the jailhouse witnesses Vaccara Comanche and Clarence Kennedy claim.

One of the numerous reasons Tony was denied a fair trial was that none of the witness statements were provided to the defense before trial. Only after the proceedings had begun did Tony's attorney receive them—and he was allowed just twenty minutes to read, including the recorded statement of the jailhouse witnesses. Twenty minutes to absorb claims, identify dates, and prepare questions that could shape the rest of Tony's life.

Those pages held the only timeline the defense could test. Without the specific dates in those statements, counsel had no way to request the jail's recreation yard logs or to line up Tony's phone records, both of which were routine, timestamped, and capable of telling an objective story. Tony called his family often; every call was logged. The recreation yard was monitored like everything else inside: names, times, in and out. But evidence that cannot be reached in time is evidence that cannot be used.

The disadvantage had begun well before that twenty minute window. Crimescene DNA and fingerprint evidence were not provided to the defense, leaving science outside the door while speculation walked into court. When the jailhouse witness took the stand, his story hinged on "certain dates"—dates the defense learned only as the clock was already running. Twenty minutes is not investigation; it is triage. Counsel flipped through pages where a strategy should have been, racing a second hand that refused to slow.

Throughout the proceedings, the jury never heard about the documented hostility between Tony and Glen Nelson because the court did not permit the defense to raise Nelson at all. As a result, jurors were unaware that, just two months before the triple homicide, Nelson had allegedly fired shots at Tony, and that even Detective Harris acknowledged the two were "on the outs." The same blind spot applied to Clarence Kennedy: both Nelson and Kennedy had a wellknown history of animosity toward Tony—context the jury needed but never received.

The jailhouse informants came up with a double-edge plan to get Tony Hunter once and for all. The other edge was that they would be able to get themselves a "sweetheart deal" on the charges they were faced with. Their objective was always to get their charges dismissed, charges reduced, or sentencing minimized. The State "hired" three jailhouse informants who would say anything to save themselves. It's critical for you to understand that the testimony used against Tony should never have been accepted as credible evidence in Court.

The jury was never told that Keith Norman was the last known person to possess the murder weapon. Cory Smith disclosed this crucial fact before trial, and it was documented on February 20, 2004. Yet it was omitted from his testimony, and the prosecution withheld this exculpatory evidence until after the trial and conviction.

> *[Handwritten note, dated 11:00 AM:]*
>
> Mike, made contact with Cory Smith. He said he could not remember the exact date the gun was stolen however, he said the night the gun was stolen he was arrested for fighting at the Library Lounge and that was the night the gun come up missing. Cory said he gave the keys to his truck to Keith Noenow (knew) so it wouldn't be left in the parking lot. Cory said he believes Keith Noenow traded the gun for drugs. Cory noticed the gun missing next day after his arrest when he checked the glove box of his vehicle. Cory said the gun along with other items were missing.
>
> Cory Smith was arrested at 5203 Desiard, Library Lounge on 1/11/01 approx 1:07 AM. MPD report attached. (Case # 01-00771)

Tony was trapped by a justice system that had systematically blocked every opportunity to prove his innocence to the jury. This book aims to share the truth of his innocence and the grave injustices that occur in Louisiana when unreliable jailhouse testimonies are allowed to shape a case. Its goal is to ensure that you hear Tony's story—plainly and fully—and understand what he has endured and what he still faces. If his story moves you, here are simple ways to stand with Tony and make a direct, practical difference:

Adding Funds to Louisiana DOC commissary. Please direct deposits to **Tony Hunter (DOC #333814)**. Commissary support enables him to purchase healthier staples in a setting where trays are often heavy on starch and sugar, with no fruit and usually only one vegetable and one meat serving per week. Including his DOC number with any contribution ensures the funds reach his account.

Contribute to the legal defense fund. Donations help cover records requests, transcripts, investigator time, and filings that push this case forward. You can donate here: **https://www.givesendgo.com/free-tony-hunter**

Buy and Share the Book

Free Tony Hunter #333814 is available on Amazon. Purchasing a copy—and encourage others to do the same—spreads the truth to new readers and grows awareness of his case.

Tell a Friend

If a donation isn't possible right now, you can still make a real difference: recommend the book, share Tony's story, pass along the legal fund link, and share **InnocentManConvicted.com** so others can follow updates. Awareness builds momentum; every share widens the circle of support.

Thank you for helping ensure Tony has the nutrition, resources, and advocacy he needs while he continues the fight to clear his name.

CHAPTER 8

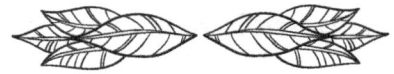

PROSECUTION CLOSING ARGUMENT

This chapter reprints the official trial transcript. Wording and grammar errors have been intentionally preserved to reflect what occurred in court.

Good morning. I'm tired, and I know y'all are probably tired too. I've been straight forward from my opening statement through my case, and I'm going to be straight forward now, and I'm not going to spend a lot of time with you. Tony Hunter is a cold, calculating, and to some extent a very smart murderer. Levi Williams, also known as "Chico" was killed because "Trigger" wanted something. Chavez and Jeremy Staten were killed because they were there and they could Identify "Trigger," and they weren't supposed to be there. All three were executed.

Once we get through with all our argument the Judge is going to read you a set of jury instructions, and I'm not going to go through all those. I may mention one or two. But, in those when it talks about second degree murder I suspect the instructions are going to tell you that second degree murder is the killing of a human being when a person has specific intent to kill or to inflict great bodily harm. And he'll also describe to you what specific intent is. And then he'll say, "In order to find Tony Hunter guilty," let's say of the second degree murder of Chavez Staten, "you'll have to find that (1) he killed Chavez Staten when he had specific intent to kill and to—or inflict great bodily harm." You won't hear anything in that definition about premeditation or malice of forethought. I don't want you to get confused in the argument did Tony go to the house to kill these two kids. I suggest to you the evidence doesn't show that. But, when Tony Hunter pulled the trigger that sent the bullet through their brain, I suggest to you that that's clear specific intent to kill or to inflict great bodily harm. As I said in the opening, and I want y'all to remember what I said earlier and what was also said by Mr. Johnson earlier and weigh that in what evidence you actually heard in this trial.

The deputies were summoned to 221 Greenwood sometime around 12:30 in the morning. The first thing they see when they drive up is a man standing outside with what turns out to be a .45 caliber bullet pistol. And during the course of the trial we now know that that had nothing to do with the crime. Deputies went inside and there were three victims, two of them still alive, one of them dead. The mother of one of these children was sitting next to him. And there's been evidence that there had been other people in the house. I—There have been, which really doesn't have a whole lot to do with this case.

The crime scene unit came and they did their job. They searched for potential evidence. They found no physical evidence at the scene that turned out to be potential other than bullets, bullet casings and live rounds. They explained to you that they looked for prints, but they found none that were usable. That they looked for hair fibers and other items but they found none. There were no tire prints to cake cast of. There were no footprints to take cast of. All they had was a scene in which obviously several rounds of pistols had been shot. The front door was busted in, and there were three victims.

The police doing what they should do they sent out a BOLO for any .22's and they found one. About a week later Monroe P.D. found it on the—in the median of 165. Y'all heard all that. Turns out this is the murder weapon. But, again, there was no usable prints on there to trace it to Tony Hunter. There was an opening of a club and there were a lot of people that went to the club and people left the house. I'm just not going to go through all that. Y'all heard it. Y'all understand that. And, listen, y'all may be mad at some people other than the person on trial from what y'all heard. And from what y'all heard you may be justified. But, again, it does not have anything to do with this trial.

At this point in time the Ouachita Parish Sheriff's Office had what we would refer to as a clean crime scene and three victims. And so they start doing everything they can to develop a case. They canvas the neighborhood, but nobody wants to talk to them. But they have one piece of evidence. Emma Rodgers, who was going home from work to pick up her kids, saw a red pickup truck driving slowly down Greenwood, according to her with a light out and with tinted windows. You saw the photos of the truck. You draw your own conclusions from it. In further looking into this you find— you also heard that the police found out that Tony Hunter came in contact with a deputy in this same subdivision about 10:40 at night three days prior to the killings, driving this same red truck. I suggest to you he was casing the house he planned to go in and rob. He was trying to see who was going to be there, or who's going to be out in the neighborhood during the time frame he planned to go back to commit this crime.

You also heard the testimony that almost two months later, after the crime was committed, that the police got Tony Hunter's truck. And at the time they got it they processed it and almost two months later they found nothing in the truck that they could link to 221 Greenwood. You also heard the evidence that almost two months later there was not a headlight out. You're free to draw whatever conclusions you want to about that. So, at this time the police, having done everything they could, as I told you in opening basically it hit a brick wall. But, "Trigger" wasn't as smart as he wants y'all to think. He thought the police knew too much. That they knew more than they should. And so he starts trying to find out what happened to the .22. Where did it go? He's concerned that he may have forgotten about something in what he otherwise thought was the perfect killing. From those attempts and those conversations you heard the evidence that placed Tony Hunter, not only at the residence, in the residence at 221 Greenwood, but also the evidence that shows he killed these people.

Again, I'm a straightforward person, and I'm not trying to hide anything from you. Were there drugs being dealt out of 221 Greenwood. Possibly. If so would there probably be drugs or money or would "Trigger" think there would be drugs or money there? Probably. And did he go to get those? Absolutely. And Chico died because of it? Absolutely. And these two children who just happened to be there? Remember this, they were not supposed to be there. But, they were. They saw him, they could identify him, and he eliminated all witnesses.

Again, the Judge in his jury instructions—They're lengthy. We apologize but that's the way the law says they have to be to define everything. The judge is going to talk about what your duties are in this case. He's going to talk to you about credibility of witnesses, and there's several sentences in this paragraph. It boils down to this, ladies and gentlemen, it's up to you to believe or disbelieve anybody you want to. It's up to you to evaluate the evidence and render a verdict in this case.

The evidence that's [been] shown you in this case, that Tony Hunter is a cold, calculation, and a very smart killer. I'm asking you to convict him of it. Thank you.

CHAPTER 9

DEFENSE CLOSING ARGUMENT

This chapter reprints the official trial transcript. Wording and grammar errors have been intentionally preserved to reflect what occurred in court.

May it please the Court, Judge Manning, the court's personnel, counsel for the State, co-counsel, Mr. Manning, the accused Mr. Hunter, ladies and gentlemen of the jury. Good morning. Before I begin my closing remarks to you I feel like I would [be remiss] in my duties if I didn't take this opportunity on behalf of the Court, the court's personnel, the State, co-counsel and the defense and the entire criminal justice system to thank you, each of you for your service on this jury, and for the undivided time and attention that you've given to the trial of this case. In a short while you will retire through that door to deliberate your verdict in this case. Before you do so I too on behalf of the accused Tony Hunter would like to review and highlight with you the law and some of the more important evidence that you have heard during the course of this trial, with the objective in mind of seeing to it whether the State of Louisiana has met its burden of proof.

Before I get to my review and analysis of the law and the evidence in this case, I'd like to make four preliminary points that I'd ask that you keep in mind throughout your deliberations. The first point that I ask that you remember and keep in mind in this case is that the State and the State alone has the burden of proof. The defendant, as you know, is presumed innocent. Stated another way, it means that he is considered in the eyes of the law as not having committed these crimes. And the burden [rests] solely and entirely on the shoulder of the State to prove his guilt beyond a reasonable doubt. Further the defendant enjoys a Fifth Amendment privilege, as you all will recall. We discussed that during the voir dire phase of the trial, and of course the Judge has told you about the accused Fifth Amendment Privilege and no doubt will tell you again at the close of the case in his charge. That is the same right that you or members of your family would have if you were here or they were here and they were on trial in this case for the very same offenses that Mr. Hunter is charged with.

Now, given that right the law states that the accused [may] rest on that right. And we did in this case. And the judge will tell you in his charge at the end of the case, that no presumption of guilt, no inference of guilt, no thoughts whatsoever concerning whether the accused did anything may be drawn from the fact that he did not testify. He relied upon a right, a constitutional right both State and Federal that you or a member of your family would have, or I would have if they were on trial here today. And the fact that he exercised that right cannot and should not be held against him. You all told me, ladies and gentlemen, during the voir dire phase of the trial that you believed the oath was sacred. That you believed that oath was serious and that they were sovereign. You also told me that you would [accept] and then follow the law. The Judge will tell you that the law is that the accused is presumed innocent, and that he does not have to take the witness stand and testify. And that no presumption of guilt or no negative thoughts can be gleaned from that. And I consider you to be men and women of your word and that you will accept and follow the law as given to you by the Court.

Now, it also follows in sequence that if the accused is presumed innocent and has a Fifth Amendment privilege not to testify that he doesn't have to present any evidence. But none the less we did present some evidence in this case, and we will go over that evidence in a short while. But I want you to keep in mind, ladies and gentlemen, that the fact that we did not present the accused cannot and should not be held against him. [I'd] ask you keep that in mind throughout your deliberations. And, further, keep in mind that the State and the State alone has the burden of proof. The defendant has no burden of proof whatsoever. The State must prove each and every element of each and every crime that is listen in the Bill of Indictment before you can return a verdict in this particular case. Each of you during the voir dire phase of this trial told me that you would require that the State prove each and every element of the crime beyond a reasonable doubt. You told me as men and women of your word that even where the evidence showed a probability of guilt, but yet it failed to establish guilt beyond a reasonable doubt, that you would not have any problems whatsoever in returning a verdict of not guilty. You told me that it would not bother your conscience any. You told me that you'd be able to go back home, face your loved ones, face your family members, face your co-workers, face the community, face the world knowing that you've been a part of a jury that found a man not guilty when you felt in your heart and in your mind, based upon what you had seen and based upon what you had heard in this courtroom that the accused was not guilty, and I believe that…you're men and women of your word and that you will keep that, ladies and gentlemen, and remember that the accused does not have to present any evidence and the sole burden is on the State to prove his guilt beyond a reasonable doubt. That completes Point One.

The second point that I want to make before I get to my analysis of the law and the evidence in this case is with regard to the evidence. As jurors you are the sole judges of the law and the evidence in this case. The Judge will tell you that you decide what weight and what credibility, if any, to give to any witness that has testified either for the State or for the defense. You can accept all of what a witness has to say. Reject all of what a witness has to say. Accept it in part or accept it or not accept it at all. That's your prerogative. That's your duty. That's your responsibility because you decide the facts, the law and the evidence in this particular case.

The Judge will further tell you that if you believe that any witness has taken that witness stand and testified falsely as to any material facts in this case, then you are justified in disbelieving such a witness as having proved nothing in this case. The Judge will tell you that, ladies and gentlemen. I want to discuss that a little further later on. Now, with respect to the evidence in this case you noticed, and as we talked during the voir dire the government presented more evidence than the accused. That's because the government had the burden of proof. And invariably since they have the burden of proof, they're going to present more physical evidence, they're going to present more testimonial evidence. But what must you do as jurors in this case? Do you count items of physical evidence and then make a decision? Do you count the number of live witnesses that were called and then make a decision? No. What you do, ladies and gentlemen, is you weigh and consider what each witness has to say, and you compare that to your logic, your common sense and your everyday life experiences. And when you retire to deliberate your verdict I ask that you keep these two thoughts in mind when you evaluate and assess the credibility of the live testimony that you heard from that witness stand. One, ask yourself this question. Is the storyteller somebody I can believe? Two. Does what he says or what he said from that witness stand make sense in light of the circumstances of this case? My common sense, my intelligence and my everyday life experience. [I] ask that you apply that test to the witnesses that you have heard in this particular case, and we'll talk about that more at length in just a moment.

Now, I only get—That concludes my second point. The third point [I] want to point out to you here, ladies and gentlemen, is that I only get one opportunity to come before you and speak to you during this phase of the trial. Because the State has the burden of proof, they get an opportunity to rebut or answer any argument that I may give. My only point here on this particular point is that I ask that you keep an open mind and weigh and consider what both of us have to say, notwithstanding the fact that I don't get an opportunity to come back before you after Mr. Ruddick—after I sit down. But Mr. Ruddick will. So, please, understand that if I could, I would. Unfortunately, the law does not give me the right to do that. That concludes my third point.

The fourth point that I want to make to you is as the Court stated during its opening or preliminary remarks to you, at the very beginning of this trial. The opening statements and the closing arguments are the summation of the lawyers. [It] is not and cannot be considered by you as evidence. You noticed when Mr. Ruddick came before you in his initial opening remarks he was not sworn as a witness in this case. When I came before you to deliver my closing remarks I was not sworn as a witness in this case. And that's for a very simple reason. We're not witnesses in this case. But merely advocates for our respective clients. In this case Mr. Ruddick and the rest of the prosecution team on behalf of the State, and myself and Mr. Manning on behalf of the accused, Mr. Hunter, in this case. Therefore, nothing that we say here is or should be considered by you as evidence. You may consider it as food for thought in assessing the evidence that you heard from that witness stand, and the items of physical evidence that you evaluated once the Judge allowed you to go down those rows and those rows over there to look at that evidence. You may consider that. But nothing that Mr. Ruddick has said before me or anything that Mr. Ruddick may say after me is or should be considered by you as evidence. I ask that you remember we're merely advocates for our respective clients and not witnesses in this particular case. Further, before I leave my preliminary points, I want to stress to you this too. The Bill of Indictment that has been filed against Mr. Hunter is not and should not be considered by you as evidence. In Louisiana there are three methods by which a criminal prosecution may be instituted. [One] of which is a Bill of Indictment, which is nothing more or less than a written accusation of guilt signed by the grand jury foreperson and filed into court in order to initiate or start a criminal proceeding. It is not and should not be considered by you as evidence. The only evidence, ladies and gentlemen, or lack of evidence that you can consider in this case is the live testimonial evidence that came to you from that witness stand, and the various items of physical evidence that were offered and introduced by the State and the defense during the course of this trial.

That basically, ladies and gentlemen, concludes my preliminary points. Now, let's talk about the law and the evidence in this case. As you all know the accused is charged with three counts of second-degree murder, one count of armed robbery. [I] want to touch on the armed robbery first and then we'll get to the various counts—other counts that are mentioned in the Bill of Indictment. The law defines armed robbery as the taking of anything of value from the person of another or that which is within his immediate control through the use of force or intimidation while armed with a dangerous weapon. There has been not one cent, not one iota, not one smidgen of evidence from any of these witnesses in this case, ladies and gentlemen, that the accused, Tony Hunter, robbed anybody in this case. You heard from a number of law enforcement witnesses. First of all, you heard from several members of the family who lived in this home. You heard from Henry Staten. You heard from Douglas Simons. You heard from Emma Rodgers. You heard from a number of people. Not—There was no direct testimony. No eyewitness testimony that Tony Hunter robbed or took anything from anybody. And, further, there was no circumstantial evidence that he robbed or took anything from anybody. What law enforcement officer took this witness stand and testified under oath unequivocally or clearly that during the course of the investigation they received information that Tony Hunter took a quarter, a penny or dollar, anything? None of them ever said that. Prosecution never asked the question; witness never gave the response. The Judge will tell you, ladies and gentlemen, you are bound by the law from going—You cannot go beyond the evidence to seek for extraneous or outside reasons upon which to convict the accused. You must restrict your deliberations. You must restrict your consideration of the case to the law and the evidence that you heard from that witness stand. There's been absolutely no evidence presented on the part of the prosecution that the accused, Tony Hunter, robbed anybody. Nothing from law enforcement. Detective Medaries, Captain Harris, any of the other witnesses that testified in this case. None of those stated that Tony Hunter went into 221 Greenwood Drive and took anything.

The other witnesses that you heard from in this case, in addition to the detectives, did any of them tell you that Tony Hunter went into the residence and took anything? They may have said something about, "well, the objective was to rob," but did anyone say that he specifically took anything? And if they did say he'd taken—took anything, what did they say he took? Did they say he took money? Did they say he took drugs? Did they say he took anything else of value? Their testimony was general and not detailed. They talked about or mentioned that there might have been a robbery. But nobody said that anything was specifically taken. And you have not been presented with any proof of the alleged robbery. Any money, any property or anything else for that matter. We submit to you that the evidence has proved beyond a reasonable doubt that Tony Hunter did not rob anybody. There's no evidence in the record to support that charge. We ask that you find him not guilty on that charge.

Now, let's talk about the counts of murder in this case. I know this is a difficult case for you, ladies and gentlemen, when it comes to murder. You look at the photographs. You become emotionally stirred. That's a natural and a normal human reaction in a situation like this. But I ask you, ladies and gentlemen, not to allow your natural and normal emotions to rial you or stir you to the point that it darkens your understanding about what took place in this courtroom. That it clouds your vision and that it drives truth and justice from this case in terms of what actually happened in this courtroom. Not what you might have heard on the streets, or the way you think the public ought to decide this case. I ask that you not decide this case based upon your emotions, not based upon your feelings of sympathy for either the State or the defense. But restrict your deliberations and your consideration to the law and the evidence that you heard in this courtroom. It's unpleasant to look at pictures of dead people, even at funerals. It's unpleasant and I know that, and I understand that. But I ask that you not be so overwhelmed by that, that you forget about your duties and not perform those duties the way that you should in this particular case in arriving at a fair and just verdict, that does justice not only to the State, but also to the accused in this particular case. I ask that you not just look at the photographs in this case and just say, "that's it," without considering what the other witnesses had to say in this case. I'm going to talk about that in a minute. If you—As we discussed during the voir dire, if you were going to just decide this case on the basis of the photographs that you saw, and the other evidence, there would be no need to present any other evidence, and it wouldn't be fair to anybody, particularly [the] accused. If that's the way our system of justice worked then the only thing the prosecution would have to do is come in here, submit to you the photographs and say, "see, I told you. We got all these dead people; we want you to convict just based upon that." That wouldn't be right. That wouldn't be fair. And if you were similar situated as Mr. Hunter is in this case, you wouldn't want anybody to do that to you. Nor would you want that done to a family member of yours. You would want to go further. You'd want to consider everything in this case. You'd want to consider every piece of evidence. You'd want to listen to what every witness had to say, because this is an important decision and you cannot just base your decision on photographs alone because that would be a violation of your oath and that would be a violation of the law in this case if you just did that alone without considering other evidence that you have heard on the question of guilt or innocence.

Now, the evidence in this case Mr. Ruddick stated that there was an opening of a club that night by Mr. Anthony Rodgers. The evidence Reveals that there were persons who were left at the house. Mr. Rodgers left at some point; other people left and joined him at that club. At some point during the course of the night someone was sent out to get some change. That was Douglas Simons. Mr. Simons was unable to get the change. Later on, Mr. Levi Williams was sent out to get change. The interesting point about that, ladies and gentlemen, is this. No one has come forward, and you listened to all the investigators in this case, to say that they observed Tony Hunter at the Club Daddy's that Mr. Rodgers was opening up that night. No one has come forward to say that after Chico left the club that night that they observed a red Ford F150, you know, ease out of the parking lot and follow him over to 221 Greenwood Drive. Nobody has said that ladies and gentlemen. Nobody has come forward and said, any of the neighbors. I submit to you that in the Tanglewood Heights area there are a lot of people who live in that area that are constantly walking the streets all times of night. Lot of people out there walk the streets at times at night, various times of the night. Now, I submit to you, ladies and gentlemen, that if they had observed [the] red Ford pickup truck circling the block, casing the house, somebody might have come forward and reported that. But they didn't. No one saw Tony Hunter at the club that night. No one saw Tony Hunter leave the club and follow Chico to the house. And you have to ask yourself this question. If Douglas Simons had gotten the change Chico would never have left the club. Never had left the club. It was purely by chance or spontaneousness that Chico was asked to go home and get change. This was not something that was planned or deliberate. Douglas couldn't get it then, so Anthony says, "all right. Well, I'll send Chico." So, he sends Levi.

Now, is there any evidence that Mr. Hunter was anywhere in the vicinity…when Mr. Williams left the club to go to pick up the change? No. Any evidence that Mr. Hunter followed him to that location for any purpose or reason? No. Any evidence that Tony Hunter was circling the neighborhood waiting on somebody to get home and then go over there and commit these crimes? No. No one testified to that from the witness stand. Detective Medaries. Sargent—excuse me, Sargent Medaries, Captain Harris, none of the other officers testified to that. When Chico gets to the house he goes in and I submit to you that he was armed with a weapon. He had his own weapon. The evidence clearly demonstrates that. You heard from Douglas Simons, indicated he carried a weapon. You heard from Harold Black that he carried a weapon. Now he's a very interesting person. Mr. Harold Black left the club sometime between 11:00 and 12:00, around the time that Chico left. He said he went to go get something to eat and then he returned. And where did he go to get something to eat? He went to go get something to eat on 165. Where was the murder weapon in this case found? He went—he went—he says he went to Wendy's or someplace right there on 165 to get something to eat. Where was the murder weapon in this case found? 165. Mr. Ruddick says, "you know, Tony Hunter is a cold, calculated, smart murderer." Well, I submit to you, ladies and gentlemen, if you're as cold, calculated, and smart as Mr. Ruddick represents, first thing you wouldn't do is take the murder weapon that you just used to go kill somebody with and throw it right out on 165 where everybody and their mama and their daddy and their brother is going to find it. I'm going to take—You know, if that happened, if you—if you're so smart, you're so cold, you're so callus, the first thing you're not going to do is take a .22 that you just used to kill somebody with and throw it out on 165. I submit to you you've got thousands of people to pass up and down 165 on a daily basis. The probability of somebody finding that weapon is certain. Smart, cold-blooded so-called killers, that Mr. Ruddick says, don't do that. They would not have done that.

Now, what that sounds like is the action of an amateur. Sounds like the actions of somebody who just got in the game on this type [of] thing. It certainly [is] not the action of a cold blooded, smart, calculated killer. You don't throw the murder weapon where on stage. You kill somebody in order to throw—throw the murder weapon on the stage. Oh, yeah. They not going to find it. Surely, they were going to find it on 165 if they weren't going to find it anywhere else. He didn't throw it out in the woods. He didn't throw it in the river. He allegedly threw it, somebody threw it, just threw it out of the car right there on 165 for the whole world to see and for the whole world to find. It's not the actions of a cold, calculated, so-called smart killer that Mr. Ruddick describes in his statements to you. And after all, what we say here is not evidence.

But let's go on. Mr. Black goes [and] gets his food, comes back. Realize this, Mr. Black lived in that residence. He moved out. Of course he says, "well I did move out." And then I ask him, "well, why did you move out?" You recall, "why did you move out?" I asked him whether he moved out because of drugs. Mr. Ruddick states that [there was] some drug dealing going on at 221 Greenwood Drive. He says you make that judgment. You heard the evidence. You heard Harold Black too. Harold Black first said he didn't move out because of drugs, and then I reminded him—

By Mr. Johnson: May I see D-3?

By The Reporter: The evidence is given to Mr. Johnson

Ladies and gentlemen, this is a copy of a piece of evidence that was introduced in the case of the State of Louisiana versus Tony Hunter. I reminded Mr. Harold Black of the statement that he gave to the officers shortly after these events occurred. And I read this to him. "Why did you move out?" Harold Black's response, "well, cause I mean it's nothing, but guys stay there, and then because of the drugs. I tell you the truth about that, this situation with drugs. I didn't feel comfortable there, you know." "Did you feel like the police might come in there any minute and you—you'd go to jail?" Harold Black, "That—That's what I felt. Yes. Yes, sir. That's the truth. That's what I felt. And I'm not trying to live my life in that position and get caught up in—in there. So, I'm like, let me back off while I know I still can." And Medaries, "now, we've been told by several people that there was dealing drugs and they—there was a possible—there was a good amount of drugs in the house. Is that—Is that possible?" "Yes, sir." That's what Mr. Black told the officers the morning of, or shortly after these events occurred...

Did he move out based upon the drug dealing according to him that took place at that residence? The evidence certainly [suggests] that. We all know, ladies and gentlemen, that drug business is a nasty business. We all know that it's a dangerous business. We all know that where there's money and drugs that things can happen. Now, people in the neighborhood probably knew based on the evidence what was going on at that home. And there are a lot of people that probably knew that. A lot of people had a reason if there was drug dealing. It's logical to think that there were people coming in and out of the residence making purchases, buying product. They knew what was kept there. They knew that there was money there. They also knew that there were drugs there. That's a motive and...a reason to commit these crimes. A motive and a reason to commit these crimes.

Now, in addition to the testimony of Mr. Black we heard from a number of other witnesses in this case. We heard from Emma Rodgers. Ms. Rodgers indicated that she saw a red truck on the night that she left her employ to go to her mother's residence, which is a short distance from where this incident occurred, to pick up her children. What's interesting is that she said that when she first passed by the residence, she did not notice Mr. Williams' vehicle. Shortly after that, after she went down picked up her kids and came back, all within a five-minute span of time, she did notice Mr. Williams' vehicle at the residence. She also described the type of truck that she saw. I'll allow you to rely upon your memory as relates to that truck.

You saw S-85 and you heard her testimony concerning the vehicle that she saw that night. She indicated that the vehicle had a double stack[1] of headlights. She indicated that the vehicle also had a missing headlamp, and she also indicated that, "if that was me, they would have given me a ticket for that." Meaning that headlamp was out. I ask you to look at this vehicle. Do you notice anything in S-85 that shows a headlamp is missing or that is...damaged in any way? There is no damage to the vehicle, and there's been no proof, no evidence that these headlamps had been changed at any time. We can't go outside the evidence and say, "well, he may have done this, he may have done that." What does the evidence show? The evidence shows that these lamps don't appear to have been changed at any point in time. That's what the evidence shows.

So, was Ms. Rodgers mistaken about the truck that she saw being the same truck that she later saw Tony Hunter in? The evidence certainly seems to suggest that. But you rely on your memory of what you heard. There's a big difference between having

---

1   Pickup Trucks Known for Stacked (Quad) Headlights, that could have been "shiny new" at the time of the triple homicide leave one possibility: Chevrolet / GMC Full-Size Trucks (1981–2021). From 1981 through the 2021 model year, Chevy and GMC's full-size trucks (like the Silverado and Sierra) regularly featured quad headlights stacked vertically on each side.

All other trucks were not new models. Truck Model/Series and Years with Stacked Headlights: Chevy K5 Blazer (Rounded Line)   1981–1991, Dodge Power Wagon & Related Mods 1979–1980, GMC Sprint & Caballero, Starting in 1976, and International B-Series 1959–1961

a single lamp, as S-85 has, and the double stack lamps. There's a big difference between a broken lamp and one that's not broken, and I'll let you decide for yourself what you believe or what you don't believe regarding Ms. Rodgers' testimony on that particular point.

The key evidence in this case has been the testimony of the three witnesses, Vaccara Comanche, Clarence Kennedy and Christopher Wiggins. If you take away the testimony of those witnesses…the government has proved absolutely nothing. You take those three witnesses out and the government has proved absolutely nothing. Nothing. So, the case really pivots and turns on what they had to say because no other evidence links or tends to try to link Mr. Hunter to this scene than the statements of those three witnesses.

Let's talk about Mr. Vaccara Comanche. You recall when I spoke with Mr. Comanche I asked him first of all what time of the day or evening did this happen that you supposedly overheard Tony Hunter talking to people about—Talking to Glen Nelson about this case? What was his response? Sometime around noon, sometime afternoon, sometime between 12:00 and 3:00. I know it was in the evening time. When I confronted him with his statement he changed his story. Well, his statement was different from what he told you on the witness stand. On the witness stand he said sometime after 12:00, maybe between 12:00 and 3:00, sometime that evening. When he spoke to the investigators on July the 20th, 2001, what did he tell them? He said 8:00 or 9:00 a.m. Then I asked him, I said, "well, who was present when all of this took place?"

According to Mr. Comanche, Glen Dale Nelson was involved in a card game. My client, Mr. Hunter, was at—came knocked on the window [and] told him to go get Glen. Nelson later came and they went into somebody else's cell and Nelson climbed up on the top bunk to look out to talk to Mr. Hunter and he was standing right there by his side listening to everything. Overheard the whole conversation. Then I asked him about, "well, what did you tell the police?" Well, guess what he told the police? He told the police that in the statement that he gave the police that Glen Nelson didn't know he was present. That he was hiding underneath some cover and nobody even…knew he was in the room. That's what he told the police on July the 20th, 2001. In March of 2004 he tells you that Glen Dale Nelson, that he was beside Glen Dale Nelson's side.

Now, Mr. Comanche also told you that he gave two to three recorded statements in connection with this particular case. Two to three recorded statements in connection with this case. I asked Detective Medaries, "did you take a recorded statement from Vaccara Comanche in connection with this case?" "Yes, sir. I did." "How many recorded statements did you take from Vaccara Comanche in connection with this case?" "One." I asked Captain Harris that same question, "how many recorded statements did you take from Vaccara Comanche in connection with this case?" "One." They took other statements from him on the 20th—one other statement from him on the 20th, but it had nothing to do with this case, according to the evidence. The question that I asked [him] point blank and specifically was, "how many statements did you give in connection with this case?" He said, "two or three." And you know what he's trying to do, ladies and gentlemen, based on the evidence? He was trying—Mr. Comanche was trying to explain the contradiction that I just caught him in, that being that "well, you told the jury on the witness stand that Mr. Nelson was right there by your side. That you were right beside Mr. Nelson when all—when you overheard this. But, later on in your statement that you gave to the officers three years ago, two—two to three years ago, you said that Mr. Nelson was not even present and that you were underneath the covers." "Well, I—Well, I—I gave two or three statements. I gave two or three statements. You're talking about another statement." No. I'm talking about the statement…that he gave, ladies and gentlemen, based upon the evidence in this case on July the 20th, 2001. And if there's only one statement that he gave in that statement, according to that statement Glen Nelson didn't even know he was present. He was underneath the cover hiding, and that's how he overheard it. Or supposedly overheard it. Mr. Comanche also had a talk with our investigator. What did he tell him? Told him that Mr. Williams allegedly was having a birthday party at the club that night, and that Mr. Williams, the reason that Mr. Williams was at the home was because he was returning to change clothes. Well, we all know from the evidence that that did not happen.

Mr. Comanche also said in his statement that the .22 that was used in this case was supposedly somewhere in Houston, Texas to our investigator. We all know that that's not true because that .22 was introduced as S-77 in connection with this case. Now, Mr. Comanche is a convicted burglar. He was found guilty and serving a ten-year sentence for possession of a firearm by a convicted felon, and also, he admitted on the stand that he's guilty—he's been guilty of aggravated battery. He's a three-time felon. Was he looking for help? The first thing the officer said, "yes, he was looking for help." Faced a possible multiple offender. Was looking help and wanted help. Didn't want to serve that ten years. You decide whether or not you believe Vaccara Comanche is a [credible] person when he took the witness stand and said what he said. I submit to you, ladies and gentlemen, that the evidence shows that Vaccara Comanche is not a [credible] individual and a person whom you can trust in this particular case.

Who else did we hear from? Mr. Christopher Wiggins. Mr. Wiggins first came into this courtroom. You saw him stand right there. "I don't want to testify." Later on, after discussions with the District Attorney that he initiated for some help, now he wants to testify. You saw Mr. Wiggins on the stand. The judge will tell you; you can look at a person's mannerisms, you can look at their—their body language and contact. He kept moving his head when questions were asked. I don't think it was a physical affliction. Just up there moving his head from time to time. You all watched that, and you can assess his credibility based on that and some other things in this particular case. What did Christopher Wiggins tell us? First of all, in his own statement that he gave to police, first he said, "well, did they knock on the door?" "Oh, yeah. They let them in." "No, no, no. That's not right. They kicked the door in." And then later on they pried the door open. He wasn't even consistent in his own statement. Later on in that very same statement he claims that the accused told him that he used a .38 and a 9-millimeter to commit these crimes. Later on, he claims that the accused told him that he shot Mr. Williams on the couch. And the State would have you believe, "well, you know, if there are inconsistencies they're based upon what Tony Hunter supposedly told them." Well, when you tell the truth there ain't but one way to tell the truth, and that's just to tell the truth. If it happened [to] you, you don't tell one, "well, you know, I'm—I'm going to tell this guy here—I'm going to selectively just—okay. I'm going to tell him about a .38 and a 9-millimeter. Then I'm going to run over here and tell Vaccara about a .22." No. No. What that [suggests], ladies and gentlemen, is that these gentlemen were [accustomed] to looking at the TV., reading the newspaper and chatting about this in the jail.

Now, you all might think that the biggest chat room is on the internet. Contrary. It's in these jails where they sit back and talk about everything to include their cases and everybody else's cases. Bits and pieces here. Bits and pieces there. Happens all the time. People talking about other folks' charges, what they're charged with, what they supposedly did, how they did it and so on and so forth. That happens all the time, ladies and gentlemen. And these gentlemen had an opportunity to discuss the case. They were sitting back looking at a whole bunch of time. One was looking at ten. The other was looking at twenty-five. The other ten. Long jail sentences, ladies and gentlemen, that they did not want to do. Now, how do you get out of that? Call the State and said, "hey man. I heard old boy said he did something. I heard old fellow said he did this," or "that he did that." These people have no respect for the law or you. If a lie will help them get their sentence reduced, they will do it. I submit to you that they will do it. And I submit to you that that's what happened in this case.

In the case of Clarence Kennedy, Mr. Kennedy was charged with first degree robbery. He had four felonies before he got that charge. He got a twenty-five-year sentence. Twenty years were suspended. Twenty years on a twenty-five-year sentence suspended. Did he get a deal or what? A five-time loser gets twenty years off a twenty-five-year sentence reduced. Now, well, did he get some help? You be the judge. The record speaks for itself. The evidence speaks for itself.

Did anybody corroborate what Vaccara Comanche said? Mr. Comanche said that there were other people in the room that might have overheard this, but they weren't listening or involved in the conversation as attentively as he was. Did the State produce any of those witnesses to come in here and testify that they overheard the same thing that Mr. Comanche heard? No. Did anybody overhear what Clarence Kennedy had to say? There was some gentlemen by the name of Jody Rucks that was on top bunk where the conversation was taking place. Was he subpoenaed to come in here and testify that, "yeah, I overheard the very same conversation and yes it did happen just the way Clarence Kennedy said it happened?" No.

Now, there's been much discussion about whether or not people are allowed to talk on the rec. yard. You heard Detective Harris say that when he went down to the correctional center he spoke with some guards. And he went down there, ladies and gentlemen, guess what he was looking for? He was looking to see if any of those guards saw Tony Hunter talking at a window. And what did Detective Harris tell you? He said he went down there to talk to some guards and none of them reported having seen the accused next to a window or talking to anybody. He went down there for that purpose.

So, we don't have any of the jailhouse witnesses supported by any other jailhouse witnesses on these various occasions that they heard, or information was told to them. We don't have any law enforcement people who corroborate what these people say about what they heard or did not hear as the case may be. All we have is their naked word. And it's interesting no other citizen outside these citizens in the jail, these jailhouse witnesses, have come forward in the last three years and said between May—Excuse me, March of 2001 and May 2001 that we overheard Tony Hunter say this or Tony Hunter admitted this to us. None. You heard Officer

Harris say he canvassed the whole neighborhood looking for clues, talking to witnesses. Nobody has come forward to say anything in the neighborhood that Tony Hunter told them that he committed these crimes or was involved in these crimes. The only people who have come forward are people who are in jail whose testimony is [uncredible], who are looking for a deal and don't want to serve long sentences. That's the only people who have come forward and told, and each one of them has an interest in saying whatever they said.

Let's go back to Christopher Wiggins for a moment. Mr. Wiggins is the same person who spoke to our investigator on February the 10th or the 11th. And in that discussion, you heard Mr. Wiggins, I asked him on the witness stand, "did you speak to our investigator?" "Yes, I did." "What did you tell him?" "Well, I told him the only thing I heard Tony Hunter—about Tony Hunter was when people—there was discussions through the food doors while they're passing out the food trays." "Did you tell them anything else?" "Yeah. Well, I told them that Tony Hunter never discussed his business with me or his activities." That's what he told our investigator as late as February of this year……..." That's what he told our investigator in February of this year. He didn't have to tell him. The investigator didn't twist his arm, didn't force him to say that. He told that. That's what Christopher Wiggins told him.

Ladies and gentlemen, this case boils down to the credibility of those three witnesses. There is no other evidence in this case that even slightly shows that Tony Hunter had anything to do with these homicides. And usually, Mr. Ruddick tends to discount that. But usually if a person did something of this nature, they leave a calling card. They leave some footprints, they leave some blood, they leave something. Something that you could trace to them. And the judge will tell you that in addition to all the evidence that you heard that you may consider the lack of evidence in the case.

Let's talk about that for a moment. The lack of evidence. No eyewitnesses in this case who indicated that the accused, Tony Hunter, committed these murders. No fingerprints that were found, either at the scene or in the truck link Tony Hunter to these murders. No footprints linked him to these murders. No matching tire prints or impressions at the scene anywhere link Tony Hunter to these murders. No physical evidence in this case links Tony Hunter to these murders. No murder weapon in this case links Tony Hunter to these murders. No fingerprints. We talked about the fingerprints from the weapon. No blood, no hair, no fibers in this case have linked Tony Hunter to these homicides. Now, you heard the testimony from Detective Harris that they went through that truck. They went through the truck. Now, if Mr. Hunter, let's say, had taken the truck and washed it and sanitized—tried to sanitize it to get rid of all the hairs, get rid of all the fibers that might have linked him to this case, well, we have sophisticated and high tech, you know, techniques now. You know, Luminal would have definitely helped us out there. The forensic people would have been able to put this together. [There] was absolutely no hairs, no fibers, no nothing from that truck linked Tony Hunter to this case. Nothing. Absolutely nothing. No—There was no blood, no fibers or hairs of any of the victims found in the truck that Mr. Hunter was driving. There were no hairs, no fibers or blood stains, anything found in Tony Hunter's apartment, The Colonial Manor Apartments. There's absolutely nothing, no forensic evidence in this case whatsoever to link Tony Hunter to these crimes. The only evidence that the State has that they want you to believe is the testimony of these non-credible jailhouse witnesses who are looking for a deal in order to save their own hides and avoid the time that they justly earned for the crime that they committed.

Ladies and gentlemen, I submit to you that as you look at this case, you look at all of the evidence that you have seen and you consider not only the evidence that's been admitted, but the lack of evidence. That you step back from just looking at the photographs and saying, "well, I'm just going to convict him based on the photographs." But you step back, and you dispassionately consider all of the evidence that you have heard in this case. And I submit to you, ladies and gentlemen, that after you have done that, you've weighed it and you've considered your logic, your common sense and your everyday experiences when you listened. When you consider and evaluate the witnesses that you've heard from that witness stand, that you will be convinced that the accused Tony Hunter did not commit these crimes. I ask you to return a verdict of not guilty. All of you told me during the voir dire that it wouldn't bother your conscience any. That you could go back and face your family members, the public, and that you would not be swayed by sympathy, prejudice or overwhelming emotions that you might have for either the State or the defense. That you would judge this case in the right manner and render a verdict in accordance with the law and the evidence which I submit to you, ladies and gentlemen, can only be one, finding the accused not guilty on each of these counts. I thank you for your time and your attention..

CHAPTER 10

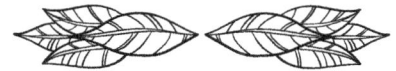

DECLARATION OF PROFESSOR ROBERT M. BLOOM

Expert in the field of jailhouse informants.

QUALIFICATIONS

I have taught at Boston College Law School since September 1973. I have been a full professor since 1994. I have also taught at Boston University School of Law, Temple University School of Law (summer abroad in Rome), University College Dublin, Trinity College Dublin, and Kwansei Gakuin Japan. My teaching includes courses in substantive criminal procedure and comparative criminal procedure. In addition, I have directed a law-school clinical program in which my student's represented indigent, criminal defendants and on sabbatical acted as prosecutors for the Commonwealth of Massachusetts. In these capacities I have handled, supervised, or consulted on hundreds of criminal cases. I have written numerous articles and five casebooks and 10 examples and explanation books.

Since 1999, I have been researching the use of informants in the criminal justice system. This has included reviewing numerous studies, investigations, and cases about informants in general, and jailhouse informants in particular. I have also interviewed judges, prosecutors, and defense attorneys regarding this issue. My publications in this area include: a book, *Ratting: Use and Abuse of Informants in the American Justice System* (Praeger, 2002); "Jailhouse Informants" in the American Bar Association (ABA) publication, *Criminal Justice* (Spring, 2003); and "What Jurors Should Know about Informants: the Need for Expert Testimony" *Mich. St. L. Rev.* 345 (2019). I have lectured on jailhouse informants at an ABA Criminal Justice Section program (Baltimore, MD, November 2005). My publications have been cited on numerous occasions.

I have been retained as an expert or consultant on the issue of informants in approximately eleven cases. I have testified in Connecticut Superior Court regarding this issue at trials on six occasions: *State v. Covington* (2016), *State v. McClendon* (2016), *State v. Lashawn* (2016), *State v. Wilson* (2017), *State v. Bruny* (2018). I have also testified in the State of Washington in 2019 in *State v. Sun* and *State v. Rivas and in 2022 State v Phelps*. I also testified on this issue in a pre-trial informant reliability hearing in *State v. Hammond* (2014) in Lexington, Kentucky. I was also prepared to testify in *U.S. v. Wells* (2019) in U.S. District Court of Alaska. In these cases, I have testified generally concerning the behavioral patterns associated with the use of criminal informants and related academic research.

I am currently a consultant to the ACLU on a case out of Orange County California on the issue of "informant tanks," where people in custody are put with informants who are likely to get information to be used at trial. I have not offered an opinion on the credibility of any particular informant in any particular case. I have tried to help the fact finder evaluate facts they should be aware of when considering the reliability of jailhouse informants in general.

JURISPRUDENTIAL CAUTION RE: JAILHOUSE INFORMANTS

Louisiana has not been exempt from the problems associated with jail house informants. In *United States v. Colomb*, 448 F.Supp.2d 750, 756 (W.D. La.2006). Federal Judge Tucker Melancon hearing a motion for new trial observed that even though he would rarely grant such a motion to set aside a guilty verdict in a criminal case and that decision should be exercised with great caution and only in exceptional cases. He ordered a new trial in this case because "Issues that have arisen in this case - before trial, during trial and after trial - are troubling. While it may not be, as argued by one of the defense lawyers, that "a cancer is growing within the incarceration system," occurrences such as occurred in this case suggest that a systemic problem may exist within the penal facilities operated by the Federal Bureau of Prisons. In the view of the trial judge, the issues raised herein are so substantial and grave that those who have the power and the authority to do so need address them."

The concerns of these distinguished judges have been borne out by DNA exonerations. Since the first DNA exoneration in 1989, there have been exonerations of people convicted of serious offenses – including those sentenced to death – in numbers never imagined before the development of DNA technology. Several studies of this phenomenon have shown that false testimony from jailhouse informants is one of the leading contributing factors of wrongful convictions across the nation. According to The Innocence Project, jailhouse informants have played a role in nearly one in five of the 367 DNA-based exoneration cases. A 2004 study conducted by Northwestern Law School's Center on Wrongful Convictions found that testimony from jailhouse or other criminal informants played a role in 45.9% of the wrongful convictions in capital cases. Today, the National Registry of Exonerations indicates that 22% of all death row exonerations were cases where the prosecution relied on at least one jailhouse informant.

Jailhouse informant testimony is notoriously unreliable because the incarcerated witnesses are strongly motivated to say what the prosecution wants in exchange for substantial benefits to themselves. Notwithstanding the inherent problems with credibility, jailhouse informant testimony is among the most persuasive to jurors because jailhouse informants typically allege to have personally heard defendants confess their guilt to the crimes charged. Introduction of a defendant's confession, from any source, can significantly bolster the prosecution's case, particularly one lacking other evidence that directly implicates the defendant in the crime. In fact, according to one study, secondary confession testimony has a greater effect on jurors than even eyewitness identifications.

INCENTIVES TO LIE AND BENEFITS

Jailhouse informants testify for benefits. The most sought-after benefits are early release and dropped charges. However, jailhouse informants have testified to seeking many other rewards within the prison system, such as more food, access to television and phones, increased visits, better work assignments and transfer to more desirable housing. Another benefit may involve help with parole hearings. In considering the benefits, it is important to be aware that jails and prisons are undesirable places by design. It is hard to imagine a greater incentive to testify falsely than a promise to get out of jail or reduce one's time in prison.

In most instances, the benefits for informant testimony are not realized until after the testimony has been given. This arrangement allows an informant to testify that there were no promises or benefits given in return for his testimony. The withholding of specific promises until after the testimony may also allow a prosecutor to avoid the disclosure requirements of *Giglio v. United States* 405 U.S. 150 (1972).

However, benefits are expected, and are realized, depending upon the helpfulness of the testimony. Everyone in the system knows how the game is played. Prosecutors and informants share a tacit understanding that the informant will ultimately be rewarded for his testimony. (*See* Michael Cassidy, *"'Soft Words of Hope': Giglio, Accomplice Witnesses, and the Problem of Implied Inducements,"* 98 NW. L. REV. 1129, 1138 n.52 (2004)). In his study of the initial 250 DNA exoneration cases, Professor Brandon Garrett discovered that jail house informants often produced "made to order" statements supporting the State's case. Few admitted they were testifying for any gain, and "[s]ome informants claimed they were testifying as public-minded citizens." Professor Garrett found that many of these informants nevertheless ultimately received favorable outcomes in their own cases. (*See* Brandon L. Garrett, *Convicting the Innocent: Where Criminal Prosecutions Go Wrong*, 124 (2011))

In recognition of this problem, in 2012 the Florida Innocence commission recommended specific provisions to Florida discovery rules to require the disclosure of informant "expectations," as well explicit promises made, in exchange for testimony. (See Florida Innocence Commission Final Report, 76-82 (June 2012) (recommending enhanced discovery regarding the State's use of informants, including the requirement that prosecution disclose "whether the informant has received, or expects to receive, anything in exchange for his or her testimony"); *In re: Amendments to Fla. Rule of Crim. Procedure 3.220.*, 140 So. 3d 538 (Fla. 2014)(adopting

Commission recommendation requiring discovery obligations specific to informants)).

Informants are also well aware that the benefits to be received will be based on the usefulness of the testimony on behalf of the State. Studies have shown that jailhouse informants can be quite resourceful in gathering the information necessary to provide "useful" testimony. For example, witnesses in LCGJ investigation described relying on media reports, having friends and relatives provide the information by attending court hearings or investigating themselves, and even impersonating a law enforcement officer over phone to tap into knowledge already in law enforcement's hands. Informants often share or exchange information they have gathered with one another. In the end, a determined informant can create a very convincing story for the jury. As one informant explained:

> [T]he jury not knowing the system of how it works is going to believe [me] when I get up there with all these details and facts that this guy sat in the jail cell, or he sat on the bus [transporting to court], or he sat in the holding tank somewhere or told me through a door or something, they're going to believe me.

Prosecutors also have incentives to rely on informants, particularly when it will shore up an otherwise weak case. Professor Yaroshefsky of the Hofstra Law School interviewed 25 former U.S Attorneys in the Southern District of New York, and sixteen defense attorneys. She discovered that prosecutors would often shape and polish the testimony of informants so as to meet with their theory of the case. (Ellen Yaroshefsky, Cooperation with Federal Prosecutors: Experiences of Truth Telling and Embellishment, 68 Fordham L. Rev. 917, 930 (1999)).

In September of 2022, I was asked to review the statements, interview reports, testimony, and criminal histories of the jailhouse informants in *State v. Tony Hunter:* Vaccara Comanche, Clarence Kennedy, Christopher Wiggins, and Glen Dale Nelson. I also reviewed several contemporaneous newspaper articles regarding the Greenwood triple homicide, and the following information.

JAILHOUSE INFORMANTS: COMANCHE, KENNEDY, WIGGINS, AND NELSON

Vaccara Comanche

July 20, 2001, Statement to OPSO

On July 20, 2001, Vaccara Comanche contacted OPSO and said he wanted to give them information on "several" homicides. He said that he had not been promised anything in exchange for his cooperation.

Comanche said that on July 17, 2001, at 8 or 9 a.m., Hunter was outside on the rec yard and asked another inmate to get Glen Dale at the window and Glen Dale didn't want to talk, and stalled, but after about fifteen minutes, he went to the POD 10 cell to talk with Hunter. Glen Dale signaled another inmate on the rec yard to get Hunter.

Comanche told investigators Nelson was on the top bunk and Comanche was on the bottom bunk when the conversation took place. Comanche stated that neither Hunter nor Nelson was aware that he was in the cell with them because he pulled in a blanket in front to the bed and turned his radio off: "It was a blanket like, ah, in front of the bed and so it was blocking me out because see, I was down there listening to the radio at first. Then when I heard them telling tell Glen Dale to come here, I pulled the plugs to my ear and turned the radio off so nobody would know that I was down there. Then they just started discussing it. He didn't know that nobody was up in the room but the person that told him that Trigger was at the window, and that was it."

Comanche said Hunter and Nelson started arguing at the window. Trigger had to "kind of shout so Glen Dale would be able to hear him." Hunter told Nelson not to tell Comanche because he didn't want anyone ratting him out. Glen said he "ain't gonna tell nobody what went on at the house." Glen asked Hunter, " who told you that I said something?"

Comanche said he heard Hunter tell Nelson not to worry about the gun, that it could not lead back to him. Comanche said Tony Hunter asked Glen Dale Nelson "what he did with the .22"

Trigger responded, "you know where it at, you know that spot, the same spot I been having for years."

Trigger asked Nelson what he told the people. Trigger asked Glen why he told the people he was at the Roderick Hall murder. Glen said "well, them people know I ain't no murderer, they know I ain't do that, I don't care – I'm just trying to get back home to my family."

According to Comanche, about the Tanglewood homicides, Hunter said, "You know I had to handle my business, wasn't supposed to be nobody in the house but Chico."

Comanche said that on July 19, the same day Comanche asked to speak to investigators, Glen Dale Nelson told him that Tony Hunter and Patrice Foy had been "at the club" and everyone was getting in for free at first, but Chico[2] didn't have any money in his pocket, so he went home to get money. Hunter and Foy followed Chico back to his house at 221 Greenwood Drive. When they got to Greenwood, Hunter pulled a gun on Chico and Chico led him to 15 lbs of marijuana and a wad of money in a rubber band that was secreted inside a hole in the wall behind a mirror. Comanche said that after the murders, Tony Hunter went back to Anthony Rodgers' club.

---

2   Douglas Simonds told investigators that Chico, Rodger's "brother," was "basically like part-owners of the club" with Anthony Rodgers. Chico certainly would not have had to pay the cover charge to get into the club.

Comanche also claimed to have heard Hunter explain to Nelson that the children were not supposed to be in the house at the time and that he had to "chase the little fu**ers around the house." Hunter "got a big knot on his head because his head hit the table chasing them" and had to shoot them "because they had seen his face."

Trial testimony

At time of his testimony, Comanche was serving a 10-year sentence for being a felon in possession of firearm. He was sentenced on February 21, 2002, to five years on a revocation of probation for Aggravated Battery, consecutive to 10 years for being a felon in possession of firearm.

Comanche testified that, after Hunter called for Nelson, Comanche followed Glen Dale Nelson into the cell because the two of them had been talking prior to Nelson being called over. Comanche testified that he climbed onto the top bunk with Nelson and was sitting right next to Glen Dale Nelson while the conversation with Tony Hunter was taking place. When asked if Hunter knew he was sitting next to Nelson during the conversation, Comanche responded, "Quite naturally. I'm sitting right beside him."

Comanche testified that there were four or five other people in the cell where he and Glen Dale Nelson were during the conversation, but they were not listening to the conversation; "they were either laying down listening to their radios or asleep."

Comanche testified that Hunter asked Glen Dale Nelson who he was "running his mouth to." Glen Dale Nelson responded "he ain't got nothing to worry about the weapon. It can't lead back to him." Comanche testified that he heard Hunter refer to the weapon as a ".22". According to Comanche, Tony Hunter said that "Chico was the only one supposed to be there" and he had to chase the kids around the house. Comanche testified that Tony told Nelson that he had to kill the kids because they "had seen his face because he had been around a couple of times and they recognized who he was." Comanche testified that the conversation between Glen Dale Nelson and Tony Hunter lasted ten minutes.

Comanche stated that he and the prosecutor had spoken about 2 weeks prior to his testimony and that he had not been promised anything in exchange for his testimony. On cross-examination, Comanche admitted that when he was interviewed by Detective Harris when he was first arrested, he had asked Harris what he could "do for him." According to Comanche, Harris told him that he "couldn't make me no promises like that. He told me that he couldn't do nothing. Only thing he could do is talk to somebody but he can't do nothing for me."

Captain Harris testified that after Comanche gave his statement to them, Comanche asked "if I cooperate, if I'm cooperative, can I get some help with my charges?" Medaries testified that Comanche asked for some "assistance" with his pending charges in exchange for his cooperation. Medaries testified that he told Comanche in response that they "couldn't give him any."

In 2014, Vaccara Comanche was using the jail phones at the Ouachita Parish Correctional Center to direct a methamphetamine conspiracy in Louisiana and Texas. He was convicted in the United States District Court for the Western District of Louisiana following a jury trial and sentenced to 151 months' imprisonment for conspiracy to possess and distribute methamphetamine. *United States v. Rogers*, 708 Fed.Appx. 178, 180 (5th Cir.2017).

Clarence Kennedy

August 20, 2001, Statement to OPSO

On August 20, 2001, Clarence Kennedy requested to talk to a deputy in reference to the triple homicide in Tanglewood. Kennedy told the investigators that around the first week of August, Kennedy was in his cell in 10C and heard someone knocking on the window of the cell. Kennedy looked out the window and saw Tony Hunter on the rec yard. Hunter told Kennedy to get Glen Dale Nelson. Kennedy said he returned to the cell laid on his bed and read his book. According to Kennedy, he got Glen Dale Nelson who jumped on the bunk bed and had a conversation with Hunter. Kennedy testified he overheard Hunter ask Nelson what he had said because "the police know too much." Hunter threatened Nelson's family and the two got into an argument. According to Kennedy, Nelson asked why Hunter shot the kids and Hunter responded:

"I had to do it man, they were not suppose to be there. Only thing we were suppose to do was rob and kill him, get the money and get the dope, and go on about your business. That's the only thing we suppose to be doing. It shocked me when I seen them. I didn't know them kids were there."

At the time of his testimony, Clarence Kennedy was housed at the Columbia Jail. Kennedy testified that he had not been promised anything in exchange for his testimony. Clarence Kennedy testified that he and Glen Dale knew each other from the street and were dating girls who were friends with each other. Kennedy testified that he and Hunter were not friends, he did not like Hunter. Kennedy denied asking the State for help with his sentence.

Trial testimony

At the time of his testimony against Tony Hunter, Clarence Kennedy was serving an illegally lenient 25-year sentence, *with 20 years suspended,* for first degree robbery in violation of La.R.S. 14:64.1. Clarence Kennedy was originally charged with armed robbery, but on February 11, 2002, he pled to a reduced charge of first-degree robbery, the state dismissed the charge of simple battery and declined to adjudicate him as a multiple offender.

Kennedy testified that while he was incarcerated at the Ouachita Correctional Center, Tony Hunter, who was out in the yard, knocked on the window and told Kennedy to get Glen Dale Nelson. Kennedy testified that Hunter was on the rec yard by himself. Kennedy testified that Nelson complied with Tony's request and when Nelson went to the window to talk, Kennedy overheard their conversation. Kennedy was on the bottom bunk and another inmate, Jody Rucks, was on the top bunk.

Kennedy testified that he specifically heard Tony ask Nelson "what did you say, because the police know too much?" He also heard him say that he was robbing the adult victim, and that the kids were not supposed to be there so he had to kill the kids. Finally, Kennedy claimed to have overheard Hunter say that there was someone acting as a lookout who was positioned outside of the house and at some point during the commission of the crime the lookout heard the children hollering and ran inside of the house. The lookout caught one of the children, and told Hunter, "you got to do them too."

Kennedy did not recall the date of this conversation, though he knew it was a on a weekday between noon and 3:00 p.m. He later claimed however, that it was "late in the evening."

Kennedy claimed that he never asked for or was offered any promise for his testimony. He testified that it "really hurt him" to hear Hunter confess to the murders, and he "thought about if it was his kid" so he contacted the investigators.

Kennedy denied telling the defense investigator that one of the deputies with whom he spoke indicated he could get some help with his sentence. Kennedy acknowledged that he was a fourth felony offender and could have been multi-billed for first degree robbery based on his prior convictions for unauthorized entry, possession of crack cocaine, receiving stolen things, and twice for unauthorized use of a moveable.

Glen Dale Nelson

Glen Dale Nelson was the inmate to whom Tony Hunter allegedly made inculpatory statements about himself regarding the March 10, 2001, triple homicide on Greenwood Drive, which was then allegedly overheard by Vaccara Comanche and Clarence Kennedy while they were all incarcerated at the Ouachita Parish Correctional Center. The OPSO Offense Report listed Glen Dale Nelson as an additional suspect in the homicides.

Prior to the Tanglewood homicides, on December 30, 2000, Glen Dale Nelson fired two shots at Tony Hunter and proceeded to flee in a brown or gold 1985 Old 98 with La Tag ILA818. On at least two separate occasions prior to the Tanglewood homicides, Glen Dale Nelson had attempted to implicate Tony Hunter in at least two other murders being investigated by the Ouachita Parish Sheriff's Office: the Roderick Hall murder and the Joseph Collins murder. Detective Harris testified at the bond hearing that Glen Dale Nelson and Tony Hunter "were on the outs." Glen Dale Nelson put Tony Hunter on his "enemies list" at Angola to prevent them being housed together.

Glen Dale Nelson was ultimately not called by the prosecution to testify at Tony Hunter's trial. Michael Ruddick, the prosecuting attorney against Tony Hunter, swore an affidavit averring that he did not call Glen Dale Nelson at Tony Hunter's trial because "he was totally unreliable, and it appeared he would say anything that he thought would help him with his various legal problems." Nelson has been deemed by multiple judges in the 4th Judicial District to be irredeemably uncredible.

Nelson's absence from the trial was glaringly conspicuous. The fact that Nelson was ultimately not called by the State to testify against Tony Hunter and to be confronted and subjected to the crucible of cross-examination to determine the reliability of claims that he held at least one, and by some accounts multiple, public conversations with Hunter in the jail about his alleged involvement in the Tanglewood homicides, did not magically excise his taint from the trial. Glen Dale Nelson remained a central figure during Tony Hunter's trial, his name was mentioned no less than 25 times, and his lack of credibility, the specter of a jailhouse con by multiple inmates to manipulate the system, in the complete absence of independent, material corroboration or physical evidence implicating Tony Hunter, succeeded in convicting an innocent man.

Glen Dale Nelson was an informant for the State dating back to at least 1992 and his longstanding cooperation and informant testimony is well known - to the Ouachita Parish District Attorney's Office, as well as to other inmates. In *State v. Hill*, Glen Dale Nelson testified for the prosecution at trial that the defendant confessed to him while both were inmates at the Ouachita Parish Correctional Center. Mr. Hill was convicted in part on the basis of Nelson's trial testimony. On appeal, Hill argued that after his arrest, he was incarcerated at the Ouachita Parish Jail for eighteen months before trial and while there, Glen Dale Nelson was housed with him for several weeks. Hill claimed that Nelson was placed in defendant's cell for the purpose of eliciting incriminating information from him for use at his trial. The defendant in *Hill* presented a witness who testified that Nelson's general reputation was that of a "snitch," but who had no personal knowledge as to whether Glen Dale Nelson was actually working as "an agent of the government." The Louisiana Supreme Court denied relief, holding that, on the record before them, Hill had failed to show "either that Nelson was an agent of the government or that the state created a situation likely to induce the defendant to make incriminating statements."

In 2000, Glen Dale Nelson was charged with having committed the murder of Roderick Hall - with Tony Hunter. A newspaper account printed in the local paper, reported that Nelson had moved to suppress his own inculpatory statements to investigators on the basis that he only made the statements because "police officers promised that he would 'walk' on the charges if he helped build a case against Tony Hunter." Nelson testified that "police were looking for evidence against Hunter, and had threatened to put the two together in a cell." On July 26, 2001, Glen Dale Nelson swore an affidavit stating that while he was incarcerated at the Ouachita Parish Correctional Center, he gave false information to Captain Harris implicating Tony Hunter in the Roderick Hall homicide "so [he] could go home." Tony Hunter was arrested for the Roderick Hall homicide, but never indicted or tried for the murder.

In *State v. Stokes*, this time the defense noticed its intention to call Glen Dale Nelson as a witness. The State moved *in limine* to preclude Nelson from testifying for the defense arguing that he was uncredible and therefore incompetent to testify as a witness. Glen Dale Nelson intended to testify that Tony Hunter had confessed to him that Hunter, and not the defendant Anthony Stokes, shot and killed the victim. Following an evidentiary hearing, this court granted the State's motion *in limine* precluding Nelson's testimony. On supervisory writs, the Louisiana Supreme Court affirmed this court's ruling, holding: "the district court judge totally discredited the testimony of Nelson. In the absence of corroborating evidence to demonstrate the trustworthiness and reliability of Nelson's testimony regarding the alleged statements made to him by Hunter, such hearsay statements are inadmissible." *State of Louisiana v. Anthony Stokes*, 2003-KK-0556 (La. 2/28/2003).

As the Louisiana Supreme Court cautioned in *Stokes*, absent "corroborating evidence to demonstrate trustworthiness and reliability," some witness testimony is so infected with manipulation that it is legally impossible to extract the truth. The virus of corruption and manipulation permeated the testimony of the jailhouse witnesses who testified for the prosecution at Tony Hunter's trial and there was no corroborating evidence to demonstrate its trustworthiness or reliability. Given the sordid history between Hunter and Nelson, and the fact that Nelson had attempted to murder Hunter two months prior to the triple homicide, it objectively strains all credibility to believe that Tony Hunter would confide in Nelson, in front of numerous additional inmate witnesses seeking to better their own circumstances, about the details of a crime for which Hunter would certainly face life imprisonment, if not the death penalty.

On January 3, 2012, Glen Dale Nelson swore an affidavit stating that Vaccara Comanche and Clarence Kennedy's testimony against Tony Hunter was false and part of a:

> "a jailhouse conning scheme organized by my friends Vaccara Comanche and Clarence Kennedy to get a conviction for the state against our enemy Tony Hunter in the triple homicide. I informed Detective David Harris that me and Tony Hunter are enemies and that I didn't know anything about the triple homicide. I did not testify because Hunter's attorneys nor investigator interviewed me about the triple homicide. If Hunter's attorney or investigator would have interviewed me about the triple homicide, I would have testified to the truth in Hunter's behalf that me and Tony Hunter have

never had a discussion about the triple homicide. It was a jailhouse con by my friends Vaccarra Comanche and Clarence Kennedy to use my name to establish their jailhouse scheme so they could get help from the District Attorney's Office for their charges."

Christopher Wiggins

August 2, 2001, Statement to OPSO

Christopher Wiggins was interviewed by Det. Medaries on August 2, 2001. Unlike Comanche and Kennedy who voluntarily provided information to investigators, Captain Harris testified that they sought Wiggins out to question him. Wiggins had been housed in a two-man isolation cell with Tony Hunter at the Ouachita Correctional Center for about two months until his transfer to Franklin Parish on July 31, 2001. According to Wiggins' statement, Tony Hunter met up with Glen Dale Nelson on the night of the Tanglewood homicides and waited in the truck while Glen Dale Nelson knocked on the door of 221 Greenwood Drive. Nelson returned to the truck and told Tony that someone was there. Tony Hunter then allegedly kicked open the front door, robbed the occupant, and then killed him. According to Wiggins, Tony Hunter was about to leave when the kids saw their faces, so he had to shoot them.

Christopher Wiggins was called as a witness by the State at trial and immediately refused to testify. The prosecutor told him that he did not have a Fifth Amendment Right not to testify. The prosecutor requested that Wiggins be held in Ouachita.

The following day, Wiggins took the stand for the prosecution. Wiggins testified that he was serving a ten-year sentence following a 2000 plea for forgery. Wiggins testified that he was in an isolation cell with Tony Hunter for 2 months. Wiggins testified that Tony told him he kicked the door in and committed a robbery in the Tanglewood area which "lead to three people being killed." Wiggins testified that Tony said "he went to rob them and the guy didn't want to, ah, show him where the drugs and money was so he shot him." Regarding the kids, Wiggins stated that "they seen his face upon him leaving out the house and he couldn't leave no witness behind so he had to kill them." Wiggins testified that Hunter told him he used a .38 and a 9 millimeter to kill the victims.

Wiggins admitted that after he was taken out of court, he asked the District Attorney's Office for leniency on his sentence. He testified that he was not promised anything in exchange for his testimony. Wiggins had previous convictions for attempted robbery and manslaughter, for which he served fifteen years. He had prior convictions for simple robbery and simple burglary. At the time of his testimony against Tony Hunter, Wiggins had five felony convictions and faced a life sentence if he was multi-billed.

The reliability problems with the jailhouse informants: Comanche, Kennedy, Wiggins, and Nelson.

They lied about the benefits they were receiving.

Each of the three jailhouse informants who testified against Tony Hunter at trial denied having been provided with any benefit in exchange for their testimony. This was not accurate. At a pretrial hearing, Tony Hunter's attorney asked the investigator if any of the jailhouse witnesses had been promised or offered anything in exchange for their cooperation and testimony. Det. Medaries responded, candidly: "We never made any promises of anything that you just described to any of those people. Frequently when you interview those inmates that… that's their motive. They may not ask you, but in their… in their mind that's … that's what they're hoping will happen."

Captain Harris testified that of the three jailhouse informants he took recorded statements from at Ouachita Parish Correctional Center, only Vaccara Comanche asked for help with his charges. Harris testified that "following the statements, he said, 'If I cooperate, if I'm cooperative can I get some help with my charges?'"

Clarence Kennedy denied having received any benefit for his testimony. In fact, Kennedy received a substantial, illegally lenient sentence pursuant to a plea deal after he agreed to testify against Tony Hunter. Kennedy was charged by a Bill of Information in Case No. 01-F0649 for Armed Robbery with a firearm of Crystal

Taylor on April 18, 2001. According to Jody Rucks, who shared a cell with Kennedy, "Clarence Kennedy told me at the time that he robbed a white lady and that he was told he would get less time for his crime if he was willing to testify against Tony Hunter. I told them both that I would not be willing to lie about this."

The Armed Robbery carried a mandatory penalty of 10 to 99 years imprisonment without the benefit of parole, probation, or suspension of sentence. As a fourth felony offender, Kennedy faced a mandatory minimum of twenty years and a maximum sentence of 198 years if convicted. Kennedy faced an additional 0-12 years on the simple burglary of a vehicle charge in Case No. 01-F0948.

On February 11, 2002, a little more than a week after the Gene Screen results were disclosed to the prosecution demonstrating negative results implicating Tony Hunter, Kennedy was permitted to plead to the reduced charge of first-degree robbery, the simple burglary charge was dismissed, and he was sentenced to serve five years of a twenty-five year sentence, with the remaining twenty years suspended. The State declined to file a multiple offender bill.

At trial, Kennedy was cross-examined about his alleged statement to a defense investigator on February 10, 2002, that he received "fifteen years in the way of help in this particular case." Considering that Kennedy was originally facing a mandatory minimum of twenty years at hard labor and received only five, it would indicate that Kennedy received at least a fifteen-year benefit.

Further complicating the issue, Kennedy's sentence for first-degree robbery of twenty-five years, with twenty years suspended, was illegally lenient and specifically prohibited by the statute. La.R.S. § 14:64.1 provides that "whoever commits the crime of first-degree robbery shall be imprisoned at hard labor for not less than three years and for not more than forty years, *without benefit of parole, probation or suspension of imposition or execution of sentence.*" (emphasis supplied).

Clarence Kennedy was apparently released onto probation with twenty years suspended, after serving the first five years of his sentence for first degree robbery. The minute entry from January 18, 2012, in Case No. 01-F-0649 indicates that Kennedy was violated on his post-sentence probation, which was thereafter extended by the trial judge. Probation is likewise not permitted for first degree robbery, by statute, and constitutes an illegally lenient sentence. A defendant has no constitutional or statutory right to an illegally lenient sentence, and such a sentence cannot stand. Pursuant to La.C.Cr.P. art. 882, a trial court is permitted to amend an illegal sentence at any time.

Kennedy adamantly denied having received any benefit in exchange for his testimony at trial. Kennedy testified that his sole reason for cooperating and testifying against Tony Hunter at trial was because it "really hurt him" to hear Hunter confess to the murders. The State did not correct Mr. Kennedy's denial, or reveal the deal he had been given, when Kennedy repeatedly denied under oath that he had received any benefit in exchange for his testimony. The State's failure to correct the record allowed Mr. Kennedy's claim that his moral righteousness compelled his testimony, to go unimpeached, and violated the state's obligations and Mr. Hunter's due process rights under *Napue v. Illinois*. When a prosecutor allows a state witness to give false testimony without correction, a conviction gained as a result of that perjured testimony must be reversed, if the witness's testimony reasonably could have affected the jury's verdict, even though the testimony may be relevant only to the credibility of the witness. Furthermore, fundamental fairness to an accused is offended "when the State, although not soliciting false evidence, allows it to go uncorrected when it appears." When false testimony has been given under such circumstances, the defendant is entitled to a new trial unless there is no reasonable likelihood that the alleged false testimony could have affected the outcome of the trial.

The grant of a new trial based upon a *Napue* **violation is proper only if: (1) the statements at issue are shown to be actually false; (2) the prosecution knew they were false; and (3) the statements were material.** In *Napue*, it was determined that the State knew that a witness lied when the witness denied that he had been promised consideration for his testimony against Napue. Thus, the first two of the above requirements were met.

The court in *Napue* further determined that "[h]ad the jury been apprised of the true facts, ... it might well have concluded that Hamer had fabricated testimony in order to curry the favor of the very representative of the State who was prosecuting the case in which Hamer was testifying ...." Thus, the *Napue* **court concluded: "As previously indicated, our own evaluation of the record here compels us to hold that the false testimony used by the State in securing the conviction of petitioner may have had an effect on the outcome of the trial. Accordingly, the judgment below must be reversed."**

Christopher Wiggins was serving a ten-year sentence for forgery at the time of his testimony against Tony Hunter. Wiggins admitted that after he was taken out of court, he asked the District Attorney's Office for leniency on his sentence. He then testified that he had not been promised anything in exchange for his testimony.

Wiggins had previously been convicted of five prior felonies, including manslaughter, at the time of his testimony and faced a life sentence if the state elected to file a multiple offender bill in his case. The State's withholding of the multiple offender adjudication, for someone serving a ten year sentence, of which Wiggins testified he was actually only serving five years, rather than serving life in prison, is clearly a sentencing benefit. Under La. R.S. 15:529.1 D(1)(a), a multiple bill may be filed against a defendant who has been convicted of a felony "at any time, either after conviction or sentence." At the time of Wiggins' testimony, the State had the discretion to file a multiple offender bill against Mr. Wiggins at any time, a reality of which he was surely aware.

The jailhouse informants' testimony that they overheard conversation(s) between Glen Dale Nelson and Tony Hunter through the window separating POD 10 from the rec yard was not materially corroborated by the evidence.

Vaccara Comanche and Clarence Kennedy testified at trial that they overheard a conversation between Tony Hunter and Glen Dale Nelson while Hunter was outside on the rec yard and Nelson was inside a POD 10 cell. Captain Baker testified that there were cameras installed on the rec yard with full coverage of the entire yard installed for the purpose of supervising the inmates. Baker testified that "anywhere from six to nine deputies" were responsible for sitting on the rec yard while inmates were out there. Captain Harris testified that he specifically checked the logs of the jail and the records and talked with officers down there and "none of the guards from our facility" could corroborate having seen Tony Hunter "talking to anybody at the window." No other inmates corroborated having seen or heard this conversation besides Comanche and Kennedy. Baker testified that a record log kept by the administration recorded times that inmates were on the yard, but neither the records, nor testimony about the records, was produced at trial.

Prior to trial, Tony Hunter's attorney filed a Motion for Jury to View the Ouachita Correctional Center. The motion argued that it was necessary for the jury to view the location where the alleged conversation took place in order to evaluate whether "due to Mr. Hunter's isolation from the general population and the construction of the Correctional Center… it is improbable that the witness[es] heard what they claim they may have heard." The motion averred that the window through which Hunter and Nelson's conversation allegedly took place, is a "protective double-plated glass window." The trial court "deferred ruling" on the motion "depending on the evidence elicited at the time of testimony as to whether this would be relevant." There is no indication in the record that the trial court ever ruled on Hunter's Motion to View the Ouachita Parish Correctional Center nor was the jury taken to view POD 10.

Willie Campbell and Keith Davis, both inmates incarcerated at the Ouachita Parish Correctional Center swore affidavits on December 2, 2022. Both inmates averred that they did not know Tony Hunter, had no interest in his case, and only volunteered to answer questions about POD 10. Both attested that they had been housed on POD 10 and swore with complete confidence, and without hesitation, that "if a person in the yard were to attempt to speak to a person in Pod 10, the two people could not communicate quietly or even discretely. Everyone, including security and others nearby could hear." Both inmates swore that the "glass in the window is really thick. You can't hear through the glass…. It would be impossible to fully understand one another if one person is in the yard and the other in Pod 10, no matter what kind of conversation you try to have."

The substance of the jailhouse informants' individual testimonies and statements against Tony Hunter lacked material corroboration, contradicted demonstrable facts related to the murders, were internally inconsistent, and contradicted each other in ways that rendered them fatally unreliable.

The timing of the conversation between Nelson and Hunter:

Comanche told investigators that the conversation he overheard between Nelson and Hunter took place on July 17, 2001, a few days before he talked to the investigators.

Kennedy approached the investigators exactly one month after Comanche. Kennedy testified that the conversation he overheard took place in early August 2001.

Comanche's location when he overheard the conversation

Comanche told the investigators that he was on the bottom bunk at the time, covered with a blanket, and Nelson and Hunter were not aware of his presence. At trial, Comanche testified that after Hunter summoned Nelson to the window, Comanche followed Nelson into the cell and sat right next to Nelson on the top bunk while he talked to Hunter. When asked at trial if Hunter knew he was sitting next to Nelson during the conversation, Comanche testified, "Quite naturally. I'm sitting right beside him."

Kennedy testified that Jody Rucks was on the top bunk when this conversation took place.

During his testimony, Clarence Kennedy testified that Jody Rucks was present in the cell where he and Glen Dale Nelson were located when he allegedly overheard a conversation between Glen Dale Nelson and Tony Hunter through the POD 10 window. According to Kennedy, Rucks was on the top bunk and Kennedy was on the bottom bunk. On cross-examination, Kennedy testified that Rucks did not have anything in his ears preventing him from hearing the conversation. Rucks did not have the cover pulled over his ears and Kennedy could clearly see Rucks' face.

Based on Kennedy's testimony at trial, Jody Rucks would have been in the same, if not a better, position to overhear Nelson and Hunter's conversation than Kennedy was.

On May 7, 2022, Jody Rucks executed an affidavit swearing, in pertinent part, that:

> In July of 2001, I was incarcerated at the Ouachita Parish Correctional Center in Louisiana. At one point, I was housed in A-Pod 10-C. At this time, I slept in an area with two bunk beds inhabited by Glen Dale Nelson, Vaccara Comanche, Clarence Kennedy and

myself. I was approached by Vaccara Comanche and asked to join a scheme that he had decided to act on against Tony Hunter, also known as Trigger, who was also incarcerated at the facility.

Further: When I was incarcerated at Ouachita, I slept as lightly as I ever had. I considered that place a dangerous place and sleeping was not safe. I would and could never have slept through an argument loud enough to be heard through the window in that area. I can't even imagine being able to hear anything outside.

I understand that Clarence Kennedy gave a statement to the police that said I was present and sleeping through this interchange between Nelson and Hunter. That is a lie, just like the lie that Vaccara Comanche asked me to tell.

Discussion of the .22 caliber semi-automatic used in the homicides

According to Comanche, Nelson and Hunter spoke about the .22 extensively. Hunter told Nelson that it was in "the same spot he been having for years."

In reality, the .22 caliber semi-automatic used in the homicides was discovered by Monroe PD about a week after the homicides, ditched as if hurriedly thrown out of a car window, on a median in a busy intersection where it was very likely to be discovered, and soon was.

Kennedy made no mention of Hunter and Nelson discussing the .22.

Wiggins testified that Hunter told him he used a .38 and a 9 millimeter to kill the victims.

Gatekeeping function of the trial court: conduct a pretrial hearing to determine reliability of jailhouse informants.

State v. Stokes

One of the measures suggested by experts to prevent a miscarriage of justice by allowing the admission of unreliable jailhouse informant testimony is for judges to exercise its gatekeeping function by conducting a pretrial hearing to determine the reliability, and therefore admissibility, of jailhouse informant testimony. Jurisdictions that regularly conduct pretrial admissibility hearings on jailhouse informant testimony have considered the following factors in evaluating the reliability of a given informant: (1) whether the informant has received or will receive anything in exchange for testifying; (2) whether the informant has testified or offered evidence in other cases and any benefit there received; (3) the specificity of the informant's testimony; (4) the manner in which the statement from the defendant was obtained; (5) the degree to which the statement can be independently corroborated;

(6) whether the informant has changed his testimony in this or any case; and (7) the informant's criminal history. After considering the evidence, the judge should determine whether the movant established the probable truthfulness of the informant's testimony. If not, the testimony should be excluded. If so, the testimony should be admitted, leaving to the jury any lingering questions on the witness's credibility.

Career snitches

Vaccara Comanche contacted Captain Harris on July 20, 2001, seeking to provide information on multiple cases.

The trial court's jury instructions failed to adequately caution the jury about how to evaluate the credibility of the jailhouse informants.

The Fifth Circuit Court of Appeals in Cervantes–Pacheco instructed that a district court "should" give a careful instruction pointing out to a jury the suspect credibility of a fact witness who has been compensated for his testimony. Subsequent cases confirm that Cervantes–Pacheco requires a specific jury instruction on the credibility of the paid witness. Although these cases primarily concern remunerated witnesses, even the Fifth Circuit has recognized that "[i]t is difficult to imagine a greater motivation to lie than the inducement of a reduced sentence."

The Louisiana Supreme Court has similarly held that a trial judge should charge the jury to regard an accomplice or informant's testimony with "great caution" when an accomplice's testimony is uncorroborated. If there is material corroboration of the accomplice or informant's testimony, the cautionary accomplice instruction is not required. Testimony is materially corroborated "if there is evidence that confirms material points in an informant's tale and confirms the defendant's identity and some relationship to the situation.

After both sides rested and closing arguments were completed, the trial court instructed the jury. Regarding witness credibility, the trial court read, in pertinent part, generalized witness credibility instructions to the jury: determining weight and credibility of evidence and bias/prejudice – discrediting testimony. The trial court instructed: "In considering the credibility of the witnesses, you may take into account the manner or demeanor of the witness on the stand, the probability of his or her statement, the interest he or she may have in the case and every other circumstance surrounding the giving of his or her testimony which may aid you in weighing his or her statements."

No cautionary instruction was given to the jury regarding the jailhouse informants' testimony. The trial court's failure to instruct the jury, in this case where the sole evidence linking Tony Hunter to the crimes was the uncorroborated testimony of jailhouse informants, to regard the testimony of Vaccara Comanche,

Clarence Kennedy, and Christopher Wiggins with "great caution" violated Mr. Hunter's right to due process and created an undue risk that an innocent man would be convicted solely on the basis of uncorroborated, unreliable snitch testimony.

To the extent that Tony Hunter was denied the effective assistance of counsel through trial counsel's failure to request a "great caution" jury instruction, Mr. Hunter is entitled to a new trial. A criminal defendant is entitled to effective assistance of counsel under the Sixth Amendment to the United States Constitution and Article I, § 13 of the Louisiana Constitution. To prove ineffective assistance **of** counsel, a defendant must show both that (1) his attorney's performance was deficient, and (2) the deficiency prejudiced him. To establish the deficiency prong of the test, the defendant must show that counsel made errors so serious that he was not functioning as the "counsel" guaranteed by the Constitution. To establish prejudice, the defendant must show that the errors were so serious that the defendant was deprived of a fair trial, a trial whose result is reliable. The defendant must prove actual prejudice before relief will be granted. In other words, he must show that but for the counsel's unprofessional errors, there is a reasonable probability the outcome of the trial would have been different.

Sworn statements from inmates in Ouachita Parish Correctional Center prove that Vaccara Comanche and Clarence Kennedy conspired to testify falsely against Tony Hunter in order to benefit themselves.

Jody Rucks, an inmate at Ouachita Correctional Center in July 2001, executed an affidavit swearing that:

> "Comanche asked me to lie. He wanted me to say that I had overheard Glen Dale Nelson and Tony Hunter arguing. He wanted me to say Hunter was outside, and Nelson was by the bunk where I had been sleeping. He wanted to lie and say that I heard them arguing about a murder. He wanted me to say that Tony and Glen Dale argued about the location of a murder weapon, about some kids who were killed who weren't supposed to be there, and he gave me more details I have forgotten."

On September 21, 2006, Rodney Gay executed an affidavit stating that while he was incarcerated at Ouachita Correctional Center from January 16, 2003, to July 22, 2003, he and other inmates plotted to give false statements against Tony Hunter regarding his involvement in the March 10, 2001, triple homicide at 221 Greenwood Drive. Gay was subpoenaed by the prosecution but refused to testify at Tony Hunter's Trial.

PROFESSOR ROBERT M. BLOOM'S CONCLUSION

Following my review of the case materials in *State v. Hunter*, it is my opinion that the circumstances—specifically the lack of external corroboration for the informants' testimony, the media contamination of the informants, the number of cases in which the informants were providing information, their status as career offenders facing lengthy sentences at the prosecution's discretion, and their perceived and/or actual incentives to provide information against Tony Hunter and to testify falsely—raise significant concerns. I conclude that these factors, combined with the prosecution's failure to give a cautionary jury instruction, created serious risks that the informants' testimony was fabricated and/or false.

CHAPTER 11

JERROLD PETERSON'S SUICIDE NOTE

State law requires that a panel of three state appellate Judges must review petitions written by inmates themselves because they cannot afford a lawyer. According to an investigative report, Judges on Louisiana Fifth Circuit Court secretly decided not to review petitions that were not written by lawyers and directed staff director Jerrold Peterson to send out cut-and-paste denials. This scheme was ongoing from 1994 until Peterson exposed it in a suicide note in 2007.

There were at least 5,000 pro-see petitions from Louisiana prisons disregarded, mostly from blacks. Peterson's death and suicide note reveals Louisiana Judges corruption in Louisiana judiciary functioning in the shadow of slavery and Jim Crow laws.

Although Tony Hunter's case was not handled in the Fifth Circuit jurisdiction and was not directly impacted by this scandal, this chapter is included to shed light on a deeper truth: the Louisiana justice system has long struggled to uphold fairness for those who need it most—especially poor Black defendants. Jerrold Peterson's suicide note is more than just the revelation of one court's misconduct. It gives voice to the quiet suffering of thousands who were denied even the chance to be heard.

Louisiana's prison legacy carries heavy shadows. For many, it has meant not just time lost behind bars, but hope lost in courtrooms. From the grounds of Angola—once a slave plantation, now the state's largest prison—the past and present often feel inseparable. The injustices exposed in Peterson's note reflect a pattern of overlooking, dismissing, or silencing people like Tony. And while Tony's case followed a different path, it unfolded within the same broader system—a system where justice can too easily depend on race, poverty, or whether someone has the right legal help.

By including this chapter, we hope not only to expose wrongdoing but to honor those whose voices were never heard. It's a reminder that behind every case number is a person—someone who matters, someone whose story deserves to be told.

Made in the USA
Coppell, TX
17 January 2026

69451826R00075